"This hopeful and honest work urges Catholics to go out and engage the secularized world they live in. Instead of lamenting the loss of past expressions of Catholic culture, Fr. Cameli sets the stage for candid conversations that employ imagination to discover what the baptized can and *ought* to do now. Deeply aware that Jesus' own Spirit guides them, their union with other committed disciples fosters a boldness that individuals alone cannot sustain. Even seemingly insignificant acts, much like Jesus' salt and yeast, make God's kingdom more visible around them. Aware of God showing the way, they can surprise the world with the profound joy that eludes so many in this secular age."

> —Elizabeth Nagel
> Professor of Biblical Studies at Mundelein Seminary
> University of Saint Mary of the Lake

"This book offers remarkable insight into how the somewhat bleak status of the Church of our times can be transformed in the future. Beginning with a fresh and thorough assessment of how the Catholic Church persists in the midst of an increasingly secular environment, Louis Cameli suggests that decline is 'what we can expect' from our present situation. This negative assessment leads the author to describe a state of affairs that requires a faith that is 'intentional, deliberate, and free,' capable of leading the Church to a renewed future. In a dynamic conclusion, Cameli proposes options that center on the Gospel, the fount and foundation of resourceful evangelization. An invitation to meet modern challenges with modern answers situates the lessons of the Gospel, the life of Christ, as the basis of response to political, economic, environmental, and sexual questions, among others. The 'Afterword' by Cardinal Blase Cupich demonstrates how 'foundational convictions,' bolstered by the teachings of Pope Francis, can lead to renewal. Ultimately, *Church, Faith, Future* offers hopeful and essential substance for anyone who cares about the Church."

> —Katarina Schuth, OSF
> Endowed Chair for the Social Scientific Study of Religion
> St. Paul Seminary School of Divinity, University of St. Thomas

Church, Faith, Future

What We Face, What We Can Do

Louis J. Cameli

Afterword by Cardinal Blase J. Cupich

LITURGICAL PRESS
Collegeville, Minnesota

www.litpress.org

2	3	4	5	6	7	8	9

Library of Congress Cataloging-in-Publication Data

Names: Cameli, Louis J. (Louis John), author.
Title: Church, faith, future : what we face, what we can do / Louis J. Cameli.
Description: Collegeville, Minnesota : Liturgical Press, [2017] | Includes bibliographical references.
Identifiers: LCCN 2016041525 (print) | LCCN 2016052033 (ebook) | ISBN 9780814645659 | ISBN 9780814645901 (ebook)
Subjects: LCSH: Church renewal. | Church renewal—Catholic Church. | Christianity—Forecasting. | Theological anthropology.
Classification: LCC BV600.3 .C357 2017 (print) | LCC BV600.3 (ebook) | DDC 262.001/7—dc23
LC record available at https://lccn.loc.gov/2016041525

To
Augustino Carley,
who brings hope to our future

Contents

Preface

History, Responsibility, and Faith

In a remote and beautiful place, I encountered a terrible story of human cruelty and—in that very same place—a legacy of extraordinary faith-filled compassion. This happened when I visited the settlement of Kalaupapa on the island of Molokai in Hawaii. There, in the nineteenth century, Fr. Damien de Veuster and Sr. Marianne Cope cared for lepers who had been isolated and abandoned by society.

Two sisters who today belong to Sr. Marianne's community led our group to Kalawao Bay on the coast of Molokai. With huge rocks jutting up from the sea, the bay is a place of incomparable beauty. Here, the sisters said, boats from the other islands would release their human cargo into the water before quickly departing. Some of the ailing people were able to swim to shore. Others, weakened by their illness, were unable, and they drowned. According to the sisters, when Fr. Damien saw that a boat was arriving he would run to the bay, go into the water, and help retrieve those who were struggling. He then brought them to a place that became their home and their *ohana* or family.

In Kalawao Bay, history tells us how human cruelty and faith-filled compassion vied with each other. That same history demonstrates how Fr. Damien's legacy of compassion prevailed.

The visit to the Kalaupapa settlement and Kalawao Bay affected me deeply. Certainly, visiting this historic place stirred many emotions in me, but it meant much more than just registering strong feelings. I became freshly aware of Jesus' call to be compassionate. I understood more clearly what Pope Francis means when he urges us "to go to the margins of society." And, very significantly, the faith history contained on this sacred ground gave me a new sense of responsibility. Somehow encountering and coming to know the faith of Fr. Damien and Sr. Marianne and the many vulnerable people in their care also gave me a sense of responsibility to share—in whatever measure was possible for me—their spirit of faith and compassion in today's world.

All of us who belong to the family of faith have had similar experiences. We encountered the faith of those who have gone before us in one form or another. Their stories not only edified or inspired us, but—even more—they brought us to a clearer sense of responsibility to share that faith now and in the future. And that relationship of history, faith, and responsibility is at the origin of the book you are now reading.

This book began with an earlier retrieval of the story of my ancestral faith. That history is contained in my earlier book, *The Archaeology of Faith: A Personal Exploration of How We Come to Believe.*[1] There, I traced the experiences of faith of my ancestors, experiences that stretched back some twenty-five hundred years. In gathering their experiences of faith into a historical narrative, I understood my personal faith in a new and fresh way. I understood that my faith has its roots in a rich matrix of history and culture and individual lives and commitments. My faith, in other words, is not mine alone. It reaches back and builds on the faith of many, many believers. It also moves forward through history with its own dynamism, as it embraces new generations century by century.

Knowing faith this way, I also recognized my part in the continuing and unfolding history of faith. I have a responsibility for the movement of faith into the future. This is no generic sense of responsibility. Because of the particular circumstances of our historical and cultural moment that I will later describe, I have an *urgent* and *focused* sense of responsibility. It is no exaggeration to say that we stand at a critical juncture that deeply challenges humanity, the church, and faith itself. Pope John XXIII captured this urgency of bringing faith to the world. He stood aware and perplexed in the middle of a century plagued by two world wars, multiple genocides, the development of the weapons of mass destruction, and the growing disparity between those who had much and those who did not even have enough to survive. When

---

[1] Louis J. Cameli, *The Archaeology of Faith: A Personal Exploration of How We Come to Believe* (Notre Dame, IN: Ave Maria Press, 2015).

he convoked the Second Vatican Council in 1961, he wrote, "Today the Church is witnessing a crisis under way within society. While humanity is on the edge of a new era, tasks of immense gravity and amplitude await the Church, as in the most tragic periods of its history. It is a question in fact of bringing the modern world into contact with the vivifying and perennial energies of the gospel."[2]

Together as the church of Jesus Christ, we celebrate a rich heritage of faith. And because of that history of faith, we who form the church and belong to the Body of Christ have great responsibilities to bring faith into the world and into the future. Immediately, however, a question arises. How shall we fulfill our responsibility? It will not happen merely with talk about it or with patchwork programs or with passively waiting for direction from on high. It will only happen when we take responsibility to look honestly and deeply at the challenges that face us today and when we take responsibility to listen attentively to the directions that God is prompting us to follow.

I make no claims to have a clear and complete answer. By no means! My hope is limited and modest. And my hope is to make a beginning. I want to encourage a conversation in which believers will identify what they have noticed about the world they live in. And then, they can also share their discernment of where God is leading his church. The conversation belongs to bishops, priests, deacons, and other recognized ecclesial ministers. The conversation also belongs more widely in the church to so many others who have "the intimate sense of spiritual realities which they experience."[3]

When that conversation takes place, it will surely spark our imagination and we will begin to see freshly what faith can mean in our circumstances. Our conversation will offer designs for believing today and tomorrow. Even more, our Spirit-guided conversation will strengthen our shared resolve and commitment to do something. And that means nothing less than bringing our faith into the future.

[2] The apostolic constitution *Humanae Salutis* (December 25, 1961), in *The Documents of Vatican II*, ed. Walter M. Abbott (New York: Guild Press, 1966), 703.

[3] *Dei Verbum* (Dogmatic Constitution on Divine Revelation) 8. Quotations from Vatican II documents are taken from Austin Flannery, ed., *Vatican Council II: The Conciliar and Postconciliar Documents* (Collegeville, MN: Liturgical Press, 2014).

Introduction

An Urgent and Necessary Reflection on Our Future

We have come to expect the unexpected from Pope Francis. Still, many people were astonished when he drew lessons from an English novel published at the beginning of the twentieth century to explain the First Book of Maccabees. The pope cited *Lord of the World* by the convert and priest Robert Hugh Benson.[1]

We have also come to expect a joyous and light demeanor from Pope Francis, and Benson's novel is anything but light and joyous. His book begins with secular currents that had taken root in the late nineteenth and early twentieth centuries. He then extrapolates these currents, projects into the future, and offers a dystopian picture of the world and the church. A thoroughly secularized world leads to an entirely reduced church and an eventual apocalyptic confrontation. Readers of *Lord of the World* complained to Benson that his vision for Christianity and the church was altogether too bleak. In response, he wrote another novel, *The Dawn of All*, which also projected into the future but very differently.[2] In *The Dawn of All*, Christianity and, more specifically, Catholicism triumph completely over the ideologies and forces of secularism. Scientism, the conviction that science and scientific method can account for everything, becomes an example of a discarded, quaint, and almost entirely forgotten way of thinking. Meanwhile, Catholic philosophy and theology reign unchallenged. Interestingly, despite a flourishing church and Catholic culture,

---

[1] Robert Hugh Benson, *Lord of the World* (London: Sir Isaac Pitman and Sons, 1907).

[2] Benson, *The Dawn of All* (St. Louis, MO: B. Herder, 1911).

1

repressive and even worldly elements in the church remain and left me uneasy with Benson's alternate vision of the future.

These novels and others like them fascinate me. Of course, part of the fascination rests with their entertainment value, but there is more than entertainment in play. I crave some way of identifying the future, as we all do. More specifically, as a priest and as someone deeply invested in the life of the church, I want to have a sense of where we are going, so that I can contribute to shaping the future of the church, which serves the coming of the reign of God.

Predictably, someone might quickly respond, "Look at the gospels. It's all there. The future is given and so is the program." In turn, I would say that it is not quite so simple, because the gospels are not one-dimensional in describing the future. We have, for example, Jesus' reassuring words of ultimate victory in John's gospel: "In the world you face persecution. But take courage; I have conquered the world!" (John 16:33). At the same time, we find these sobering words of Jesus in Luke's gospel: "when the Son of Man comes, will he find faith on earth?" (Luke 18:8). The gospels are utterly insistent on the primacy of God's unfailing grace, and they are equally insistent on human freedom, which may or may not embrace that grace. The future belongs to God, and there is no doubt about that. The future is also shaped by human responses, and there is much to doubt about that.

Identifying future trends for church and society and then developing pastoral responses to them is not a speculative exercise without practical consequence. In fact, the opposite is true. Looking into the future, as best as we can, and planning, again as best as we can, for that future is an especially urgent and practical task. Perhaps I can illustrate this from my own experience as a pastor.

I was the pastor of a parish with about twelve hundred registered households. The parish was fifty years old, very stable, and situated in a solidly middle-class outer ring of the city. Seniors were by far the largest percentage of active parishioners. I often joked that the cut-off age for our youth group was seventy-five.

During my tenure, I was able to mobilize parishioners to get the parish out of a $200,000 debt incurred after all savings had been spent down trying to maintain a school that finally closed with an enrollment of eighty-eight students representing twenty parish families. Ongoing financial support enabled us to meet our budget, but there were no margins for expanding staff or services. It was always a struggle.

Because of the number of seniors, the parish celebrated a large number of funerals and few baptisms and fewer marriages. Parishioners who died were not replaced by others. The parish seemed to shrink a bit each year. The shrinkage stood in sharp contrast to the time of the parish's establishment fifty years before, when a burgeoning Catholic population of young families filled the pews and the school. In fact, at that time other parishes also rose in the neighborhood, so that a mile and a half in every direction from my parish was another Catholic church.

Changed demographics, limited financial resources, and aging infrastructure—all these posed real and significant challenges for me, the pastor who had responsibility for guiding and sustaining the community. And yet, these challenges were by far secondary to another, deeper, and much more pressing challenge that I faced on a daily basis. I felt stymied and unprepared when I regularly encountered a bewildering range of people who made claims on the parish and on me but whose faith varied from deep to superficial to seemingly nonexistent. This was a complicated situation, and I will try to explain it as best as I can.

Overall, my parishioners were not theologically sophisticated people, but many of them—the core of the parish—were very devout, committed, and holy. They might not have been able to articulate their faith, but they lived it in such a way that they challenged me to follow Jesus more closely and more generously. For that, I shall be forever grateful. There were also other basically good people who were parishioners, but for them the parish was not first and foremost a community of faith. Rather, the parish was part of their social framework. Their participation seemed not so much rooted in convictions of faith as in the need for a stable community. Consequently, their participation in the faith and worship life of the community was often quite limited. And these parishioners mightily resisted any change that would upset their routines. A third and final group of people had little, if anything, to do with the parish. They came to request a religious service, perhaps a baptism or a funeral or a house blessing.

They seemed to be poorly catechized or even plainly uncatechized. Frequently, they had their own ideas for embellishing the church's rituals. They evinced no desire to connect with the ongoing life of the church through worship and community participation. They were focused on their specific requests, usually determined to have it their way, and generally belligerent and even hostile when challenged or invited to consider things in a different way.

Sometimes I would step back and survey the situation in the parish. I did not have a single community but multiple populations more or less connected to the faith that I was to serve in their lives. I was the one priest in the parish. And the parish itself had limited staff and financial resources. I asked myself, "Where is this going? And what am I supposed to do?" Embedded in those questions was the larger question about the future. I remember telling a priest friend, "It can't be business as usual." I meant that if we carried on, as we always had, we would spend ourselves down in money, in other resources, and in personal and spiritual energy. And, in the end, all we would have for this investment was a dismal result. No people would be around, even to turn off the lights.

The questions and the dilemmas that I faced in the parish obviously do not tell the whole story of the church. My parish was like a subatomic particle in the larger universe of the church. There are vibrant parishes with younger parishioners, for example, in the Hispanic community. And there is plenty of growth for the church in certain parts of the United States and in other parts of the world. Still, I would submit that my parish reflected many challenges that all of us face in the church in North America as we move into the future.

Although there is a wide array of parish renewal programs designed to revitalize local communities of faith, larger questions about the church's future and adequate responses to that future remain. The church's future is inextricably wound together with an ever more complex cultural and world situation. So, if we have an eye on the church's future, we also need to have an eye on the world we inhabit and the culture that gives us our context.

How can we move forward? In these reflections, I propose a number of steps that correspond to four questions. My primary focus is on the church but, as I just noted, with needed and adequate attention paid to the world and its culture. Then, the first question is, *What can we expect?* What can we expect the church to look like in a future world that is already beginning to take shape? We can draw from empirical studies, for example, sociological investigations. We can also draw from history and philosophy. We do have available data from which we can extrapolate into the future. We can identify reasonable expectations of our future and the future of the church.

The second question is a bit of a paradox, but it is very important: *Is there anything unexpected that we could possibly expect?* I mean that history teaches us that there can be surprising turns, unpredicted events, and unanticipated directions. Can we identify—just for our own reference—anything that *might* surprise us as we anticipate the future? Is there anything that might cause us to alter our projections of the future?

Once we have a sense of what to expect and what could surprise us, we will move to a third and more practical question: *What can we do?* How can we go forward now and effectively anticipate the future? What renewal and what new directions for the church will enable us to be the church that God wants us to be and that the world needs? In other words, we need to determine what options are available to us for our response to the future.

The fourth and final question invites us to make a choice. There are probably many things we *can* do but we need to pursue a final practical question: *What ought we to do?* How can we take advantage of the best possibilities for our response and our action? There may be many possibilities for what we can do, but we are finite creatures working in a limited universe. If we want to move forward effectively and well, we will narrow down our choices, discern the best option, and make a decision. Here, with the help of Cardinal Blase Cupich, we will consider the directions taken by a particular local church that is deciding how to embrace the future.

These four questions, then, give structure and direction to these reflections:

What can we expect?
Is there anything unexpected that we could possibly expect?
What can we do?
What *ought* we to do?

1

What Can We Expect?

No one can predict the future with pinpoint accuracy. Still, there are ways to read our history and our current situation to detect clues about what may lie ahead for us. And I will employ a modest method, as I explore the first question: What can we expect? What can we expect for the church whose life is intertwined with the world and the cultures in which it lives and moves?

I will use three different kinds of resources. The first is historical-philosophical reflection, and for that I will draw on Charles Taylor's book *A Secular Age*.[1] Taylor helps us to understand how a secular or this-worldly worldview has developed across the last five centuries and shaped the culture in which we currently live. The historical-philosophical dynamics continue today and so give us some sense of where we are headed.

A second resource crosses over into cultural and political analysis. Here, I draw on James Davison Hunter's study *To Change the World: The Irony, Tragedy, and Possibility of Christianity in the Late Modern World*.[2] In a cover blurb, Robert Bellah accurately describes Hunter's scope as an "analysis of culture and the capacity of Christians to influence it (or not)." This analysis reveals how Christians and the church navigate today's world and how they will navigate tomorrow's world.

---

[1] Charles Taylor, *A Secular Age* (Cambridge, MA: Harvard University Press, 2007).
[2] James Davison Hunter, *To Change the World: The Irony, Tragedy, and Possibility of Christianity in the Late Modern World* (New York: Oxford University Press, 2010).

A final set of resources comes from sociological studies. I use Robert Putnam and David Campbell's *American Grace: How Religion Divides and Unites Us* to survey today's religious landscape in the United States.[3] A more targeted sociological study, Christian Smith's *Young Catholic America: Emerging Adults In, Out Of, and Gone from the Church*, helps us draw a line from today into the future with our attention specifically focused on the Catholic Church.[4]

With these three different kinds of resources, we can connect the dots. And if we do, we arrive at a very sobering picture of the future of the church, which, of course, necessarily retains its perennial and foundational features. The church will, however, live out its identity and mission in a way that differs significantly from the way that many of us experienced earlier in our lives.

A natural question flows from this projected portrait or assessment: What shall we do? How shall we care for the church? How shall we care for people both within and without the church, as we enter the future? Those questions will occupy us in another part of our reflections. First, we need to know where we are, and then we can begin to anticipate the future.

We Live in a Secular Age Now; Can We Expect a Secular Age in Our Future?

Charles Taylor meticulously examines four centuries that culminate in our own secular age. At the beginning of his study, *A Secular Age*, he identifies the salient fact of contemporary secularism: "for the first time in history a purely self-sufficient humanism came to be a widely available option."[5] In other words, there is no need to turn to God via religion or faith to complete what might be missing from our lives. Carefully, he notes that not everyone in this secular age has embraced this purely self-sufficient humanism. It does remain, however, as "a widely available option."

---

[3] Robert D. Putnam and David E. Campbell, *American Grace: How Religion Divides and Unites Us* (New York: Simon and Schuster, 2010).

[4] Christian Smith et al., *Young Catholic America: Emerging Adults In, Out of, and Gone from the Church* (New York: Oxford University Press, 2014).

[5] Taylor, *A Secular Age*, 18.

Another way to understand this fact of secularism is in the question that Taylor raises about faith: "Why was it virtually impossible not to believe in God in, say, 1500 in our Western society, while in 2000 many of us find this not only easy, but even inescapable?"[6] Faith in secular context, in other words, unlike earlier epochs, is not automatic, not something into which we are born and then live with until we die.

Across more than eight hundred pages, Taylor explains how we have arrived at this point. A simple summary of his argument is impossible, but some of the major lines of development are important to note. For example, a fundamental trust in the sufficiency of human reason to discover truth means that taking things on faith is no longer necessary to get to reality. And although God is not entirely dismissed in the modern world, it is a particular god who remains. This is the god of Deism, a god who gets things going in the universe and then walks away. The Deist god opens the door to an impersonal universe. Effectively, this means removing God's involvement from the world and shifting attention from what God might do to what human beings, in fact, can do and are doing. In this shift, an enchanted spirit-world full of superstition vanishes and a rational world emerges, one that is amenable to taking human direction. And there are other consequences.

At a large social level, religion is delinked from society. It is no longer a source of social cohesion. In fact, because of the pluralism of beliefs in the modern world—and, one might add, the relativism that seems to be part and parcel of a secular society—tolerance of all convictions, whatever they may be, is the norm. And the only thing not tolerated is intolerance. At a personal level, if you choose to be religious, you can be religious on your own terms, because a secular age is an age of personal authenticity marked by expressive individualism and the supreme value of personal choice.

If we accept Taylor's philosophical-historical assessment of our age as a secular age, what are the implications for understanding possibilities for the life of faith and the church now and in the future? A

---

[6] Ibid., 25.

full and adequate application of Taylor's thought to fostering faith and church life today and in the future is yet to be done, and it certainly is beyond our scope here. Still, there are some important, if limited, practical conclusions that we can draw from *A Secular Age*, conclusions that might have a direct bearing on parish life and ministry.

When we see the history of secularization, especially in the last five hundred years, laid out before our eyes, we must recognize that we are not dealing with a fad or a short-term trend. The long process of secularization has enabled scientific, economic, and political developments. Secularization has enabled human beings to see what they can do and encouraged them to take up their responsibility in the world. That sense of human agency is not going away. It remains universally embedded in some form, even down to the humblest parishioners who lack the conceptual apparatus to explain the sense of possibility and freedom that belongs to them in a secular age. Consequently, believers want their faith to be reasonable, want freedom to make important decisions about their lives, and want to feel ownership for the faith communities to which they belong.

Of course, the larger secular narrative can take a nasty turn and assume a hostile stance toward faith and religious institutions. And this has happened, notably in the twentieth century with certain political movements and philosophical schools. Interestingly, these negative and hostile turns of secularization have not led the church to condemn the process. In fact, authoritative church teaching endorses good and healthy forms of secularization. The Second Vatican Council in its Pastoral Constitution on the Church in the Modern World embraces a legitimate secularization when it speaks of a "rightful autonomy of earthly affairs." For example, we read,

> If by the autonomy of earthly affairs is meant the gradual discovery, exploitation, and ordering of the laws and values of matter and society, then the demand for autonomy is perfectly in order: it is at once the claim of modern man and the desire of the creator. By the very nature of creation, material being is endowed with its own stability, truth and excellence, its own order and laws. . . . However, if by the term "autonomy of earthly affairs" is meant that material being does not depend on God and that man can use it as if it had no relation to its creator, then the falsity of such

a claim will be obvious to anyone who believes in God. Without a creator there can be no creature. . . . Once God is forgotten, the creature is lost sight of as well. (*Gaudium et Spes* 36)[7]

So, what can we expect for the future? The historical-philosophical reflections on our secular age speak about our world, a world that will be with us into the future, and about the church that journeys in that world. Secularization represents and will represent the culture that shapes our understanding, our values, and the courses of action that we pursue. The positive aspects of a secular culture include (1) an approach to faith that is deliberate and intentional; (2) a respect for reason that is entirely compatible with faith; and (3) some insurance against the manipulative use of religion for nonreligious purposes, such as the domination and exploitation of other human beings. The shadow side of secularization can also haunt the culture and the church. It takes autonomy—literally, being a law unto oneself—and absolutizes it. The transcendent dimension of existence is unacknowledged or suppressed and not allowed expression. In short, secularization is fundamentally good, although it can also be susceptible to deviations. Finally, secularization sets expectations for people, expectations that spill over into church life and trickle down to parish life and among parishioners who might find the term "secularization" entirely baffling. Without being conceptually aware of secularization, they expect and want what secularization offers, especially a certain autonomy, freedom, and ownership for institutional life.

We Believe in Transformation; Will We Change the World?

Jesus tells his followers, "You are the salt of the earth . . . You are the light of the world" (Matt 5:13-14). With those images, he gives

---

[7] These same themes have been echoed and emphasized more recently by Pope Francis in his encyclical *Laudato Sì* (On Care for Our Common Home; May 24, 2015). So, for example, he writes, "A correct relationship with the created world demands that we not weaken this social dimension of openness to others, much less the transcendent dimension of our openness to the 'Thou' of God. Our relationship with the environment can never be isolated from our relationship with others and with God. Otherwise, it would be nothing more than romantic individualism dressed up in ecological garb, locking us into a stifling immanence" (119).

his disciples an identity as agents and instruments of change and transformation. Of course, that transformation begins as personal conversion—from sinner to regenerated and forgiven child of God, and from mortal human being subject to death to coheir of eternal life with Christ. Once transformed by word, faith, and sacrament, we become responsible for the transformation of the world, as the world's salt and light. Then, we can describe—accurately but with some dose of theological jargon—the church as the transformational community of the transformed.

Scripture is clear and so is church teaching. The community of believers draws an essential dimension of its identity from its mission to foster the transformation of this world that culminates with Christ's return in glory and the definitive establishment of the reign of God. So the Second Vatican Council's Dogmatic Constitution on the Church says, "The promised and hoped for restoration, therefore, has already begun in Christ. It is carried forward in the sending of the Holy Spirit and through him continues in the Church in which, through our faith, we learn the meaning of our earthly life, while we bring to term, with hope of future good, the task allotted to us in the world by the Father, and so work out our salvation" (*Lumen Gentium* 48).

If we are to move into the future as believers and be who we are supposed to be, then we must be instruments and agents of change and transformation. In the imagination of many of our contemporaries—and this is probably also true for a good segment of believers—the church is a reservoir, a holding place, and an essentially conservative institution. In their minds, the church remains solely focused on the maintenance of doctrines, traditions, and practices rather than on changing the world. That judgment, however, represents a basic distortion of the identity of believers and the church. If the church is to remain true to itself and move into the future, it will do so as an agent and instrument of change. A serious question, however, arises when we survey the contemporary landscape. As we go into the future, can believers gathered in the church really and truly effect change? It is a question of great significance, because it touches on the central identity of believers and the church as salt and light in the world. Or will we be outside the process that actually shapes our lives and our world?

James Davison Hunter takes up this question in his book *To Change the World: The Irony, Tragedy, and Possibility of Christianity in the Late Modern World*. His book pairs well with Taylor's. The perspective that Hunter brings is cultural, social, and political.

Hunter reviews how our culture is actually shaped and changed. He also reviews how the Christian churches in the United States have largely adopted engagement in politics as the path to change, an engagement that is energized negatively by not liking what they see in the culture and, therefore, wanting "to take the culture back."

Like Charles Taylor's analysis of our secular age, Hunter's complex argument cannot be easily and quickly summarized. We can, however, name some of his important themes and conclusions. He identifies important and dominant motifs that have a direct bearing on how we understand the world and the church that lives in the world. For example, he invites us to revise our common view about culture and change by looking at a fundamental paradox embedded in our life together: "In America today, 86 to 88 percent of the people adhere to some faith commitments. And yet our culture—business culture, law and government, the academic world, popular entertainment—is intensely materialistic and secular. Only occasionally do we hear references to religious transcendence in these realms, and even these are vague, generic, and void of particularity. If culture is the accumulation of values and choices made by individuals on the basis of these values, then how is it that American public culture today is so profoundly secular in its character?"[8]

As Hunter grapples with this question, he demonstrates how, in fact, culture is shaped and changed. Culture, in the first place, is not the product of a democratic process. American culture would look very different, if it were. Cultural shifts depend on places that are strong in cultural production, for example, prestigious intellectual institutions, such as think tanks, elite academic institutions, and publishing houses, as well as high-end purveyors of the arts. Christian presence is found not among the strong culture producers but rather among the weaker ones. Furthermore, contrary to some voices of the Christian right, culture does not shift quickly. There is no turn-

---

[8] Hunter, *To Change the World*, 19.

around in a generation. Culture finds its shape and transformation across generations. The use of politics to change culture—as some Christians would have it—is doomed to failure, because it does not correspond to the dynamics of cultural change. It does not work, and Hunter does not tire of repeating this conclusion on the basis of historical data that he summons.

Hunter also highlights the contemporary Christian propensity to want to move in a new cultural direction because of *ressentiment*, that French word that captures an aggrieved and injured spirit, perhaps even a sense of being victimized. Practically, this means an inability for Christians to offer constructive, imaginative, and creative alternatives to what the current and dominant culture offers. It is impossible, in effect, to build culture on the negative identity that some Christians assume vis-à-vis the culture. At the same time, Hunter sees the real basis in the historical realities of our time for the Christian sense of injury: "The forces of secularity in contemporary America, within such institutions as higher education, public education, the news media, advertising, and popular entertainment, *are* very powerful and their agenda (deliberately or not) *is* fundamentally at odds with traditional Christian morality and spirituality. Whatever positive contributions one may find in it, much of this secularity *is* a solvent on settled convictions and ways of life. What remains of a traditional culture, therefore, *is* threatened with extinction, and Christian conservatives are right to worry about the effects of this on their descendants."[9]

Hunter's hard realism cuts both ways, when he acknowledges the hostile cultural environment that legitimately concerns committed Christians and when he affirms the relative impotence of Christians to reshape or reformulate that cultural environment to be in greater conformity with Christian vision and values. Does he propose a remedy to break through this impasse?

Before we consider Hunter's response to the split between Christian faith and secular culture as he has come to understand it, we can use his conclusions as a lens to view church life on a local level.

---

[9] Ibid., 167.

Where does his analysis leave a parish or a diocese or, for that matter, the Catholic Church in the United States? A particular image comes to my mind. It seems that these different expressions of church are bigger or smaller islands in a vast and dominant secular ocean. The islands are undeniably present in the ocean, but they are odd and eccentric spots of belief and custom. They have none of the presence of continental landmasses that can encounter and challenge the sea. In fact, they seem to be at the mercy of the ocean and always in danger of being swamped and submerged. And this fact is not lost on those who live on the islands. Many—maybe most—of these inhabitants are more shaped by the ocean that surrounds them than the island on which they live. The variance, for example, between "official church teaching" and its lack of acceptance by those who belong to the church has been a steady drumbeat of religious reporting. The reported variance often concerns the moral dimensions of human sexuality, but it is not limited to that. It might also be about economic justice, capital punishment, and even spiritual teaching on restraint in the use of the world's goods. So, where does this leave us now and into the future?

If we return to Hunter, we find not a remedy to the dilemma of Christians living in a thoroughly secularized world but a simple and straightforward response. His proposal, as I understand it, is for Christians and the Christian church to live out a theology of faithful presence. That means steadfastly maintaining Christian identity and values without compromise. It also means engaging the world "within a dialectic of affirmation and antithesis."[10] Such engagement means affirming the good that is undeniably present in the world, the same world created good by God. It also means standing antithetically to the world subject to sin and the Fall and becoming a community of resistance, as it works toward the constructive subversion of structures and frameworks that are incompatible with God's plan and design for humanity.[11]

Underlying Hunter's sense of the present and the future for Christians is his absolutely correct conviction that we do not bring

[10] Ibid., 231.
[11] Ibid., 234–35.

about the kingdom of God. On the contrary, the reign of God is the work of God taking hold of this world and transforming it. Christians in the church have a modest but important, if not decisive, role to play that is captured in Hunter's phrase "faithful presence." Within a range of witness and resistance, believers can foster those conditions that God will use to claim sovereignty in this world.

How, then, can we understand Hunter's way of seeing Christians and the church now and in the future in the context of a secular world? Hunter understands that Christians are in the world but not of the world. This condition or status is described in the well-known *Letter to Diognetus*, which he cites.[12] So, Christians are paradoxically both full-fledged citizens of the world and, simultaneously, aliens. They are at once immersed in the world's life but also detached from it. This has always been the case, and it will continue into the future. In this sense, the current questions surrounding "a secular age" are the perennial questions faced by believers in every generation.

Hunter's response of "faithful witness" suggests that those who offer the witness to the world are, indeed, faithful. They need to be true believers. They will necessarily be convinced, steadfast, and uncompromised. They will belong to a church that is the church of true believers. There is, it would seem, little room for incorporating in the church those who are anything less than real and intentional believers. And, by necessity, those believers are very consciously and deliberately formed in their faith. They know clearly who they are, and they stand out distinctly from the secular backdrop of the world in which they live.

Finally, the engagement of believers in the world is driven by "faithful presence." So, continued engagement does not depend on the success or lack of success of what believers do. In the end, God is the responsible agent for the world's transformation.

Charles Taylor's work gives us a macro-historical and philosophical view of the secular world in which we live now and for the foreseeable future. James Davison Hunter shrinks the picture. He locates Christians and the church in that secular world and identifies their mutual engagement and disengagement. The future church—it

---

[12] Ibid., 284–85.

seems from Hunter's perspective—looks smaller, clearly committed, and far more resistant than pliant to the surrounding secular culture.

How Does the Church Look in This Secular Culture and What Will It Look Like in the Future?

Charles Taylor and James Davison Hunter have provided us with a perspective on secularity. That is the context in which we live and in which the church exists. Their perspective, which is historical, philosophical, and cultural, has yielded a portrait of secularity that is our current context and, most probably, our future context as well. A next question leads us to examine the actual impact of secularity on believers and the church. How, in fact, does living in a secular age shape and affect believers and the church to which they belong? To respond to that question, we need to turn to sociological studies that sift through empirical data to obtain a sounding of the impact of a secular world on believers today and—by extrapolation—into the future.

A first sociological study to consider is by Robert Putnam and David Campbell. They look at the overall state of religion and religious belief in the United States. Their study *American Grace* is especially valuable, because it summarizes a vast quantity of empirical research. It provides a portrait and a sketch of trends for religion and religious faith in the United States.

A summary of trends across denominational lines identifies an overall decline of religious participation that will likely carry into the future. Putnam and Campbell affirm that "independent streams of evidence suggest that Americans have become somewhat less observant religiously over the last half century, mostly because of slight but cumulative declines from generation to generation."[13] The specific pattern for Catholics in the United States is even starker: "Roughly 60 percent of all Americans today who were raised in America as Catholics are no longer practicing Catholics, half of them having left the church entirely and half remaining nominally Catholic, but

---

[13] Putnam and Campbell, *American Grace*, 79–80.

rarely, if ever, taking any part in the life of the church."[14] This dismal picture of a declining Catholic population must, however, be adjusted to incorporate the influx of Latino immigrants that continues to sustain the Catholic Church in the United States as the single largest denomination in the country. The close affiliation of the Latino community with the Catholic Church, however, may loosen, as it did for other immigrant groups, when ethnic identity and religious identity become unbound from each other.

A final observation from Putnam and Campbell looks at one significant measure of the internal quality of Catholic faith by those who profess to be its adherents, that is, their conformity to what the church teaches: "As a group Latino Catholics consistently adopt a more orthodox perspective than their 'Anglo' co-religionists, although neither group could be characterized as hewing closely to the official teachings of the Catholic Church. In fact, the low percentage of Catholics who endorse orthodox Catholic doctrine is striking."[15]

In general, Putnam and Campbell offer a religious portrait of the United States that highlights a relatively high level of religiosity in a secular environment. That religiosity, however, is quite general and does not translate into consistent patterns of religious participation, for example, in the worship life of the churches. The Catholic community in the United States presents a complex picture. On the one hand, especially in the Anglo community, Catholic participation is in steady decline. The Latino community, on the other hand, boosts the overall number of participants in the church, at least for now. Still, both Anglo and Latino Catholics demonstrate a thin affiliation with their faith, as that faith is proclaimed and held by the church with regard to doctrine, moral choices, and regular participation in the life of worship. For Catholics and for the Catholic Church in the United States the overall portrait is one of loose connections. And these loose connections suggest trends that will carry into the future and probably intensify.

In addition to the Putnam and Campbell study *American Grace* with its general focus on religion in America, we are fortunate to have

[14] Ibid., 140–41.
[15] Ibid., 301.

much more targeted sociological studies of Catholic young people by Christian Smith of the University of Notre Dame and his associates. They have been tracking Catholic teenagers as they become emerging adults in their early twenties as part of the *National Study of Youth and Religion*. The particular studies that have emerged from this longitudinal perspective are extraordinarily valuable for many reasons. They identify, for example, decisive formational experiences that the church should take into account while ministering to young people. For our purposes, Christian Smith's latest study *Young Catholic America: Emerging Adults In, Out of, and Gone from the Church* (2014) enables us to see the religious development (or its lack) of young people living in a secular age. Because they are young, the trends manifested in their development today suggest important directions in the life of the church tomorrow. Their stories, in other words, can be a bellwether for the church of the future in a secular age.

Again, as with Putnam and Campbell's *American Grace*, Christian Smith's book *Young Catholic America* is not susceptible to a quick summary. He brings together a wealth of statistical data, important distinctions (such as differences in Anglo and Hispanic experience), and compelling narratives drawn from personal interviews with young people who have been involved in the study since they were thirteen years old. For our purposes, I will cite several conclusions from *Young Catholic America* to provide a sketch of challenges that the church will face. In fact, the church itself is challenged by the future that these young believers represent. Three areas are especially noteworthy: (1) Sunday Mass attendance; (2) acceptance of Catholic beliefs and values; (3) general patterns of identification and affiliation as Catholic.

Sunday Mass attendance. It is no surprise that a small percentage of Catholic emerging adults (between 10 and 20 percent) attend Sunday Mass regularly. Regular Sunday Mass attendance is an obviously important marker for belonging to and practicing the Catholic faith. Historically, adolescents slipped away from regular participation in Sunday Mass and, then, with marriage and children returned. With a careful statistical analysis of available data, Smith concludes that this pattern will not hold for the future: "Although we are not in the business of predicting the future, we doubt that today's emerging adult Catholics will substantially increase their Mass attendance as they age."[16] This tells us what lies ahead on Sunday mornings—fewer and older people at Sunday Mass. The pattern is in place now, and the *National Study of Youth and Religion* indicates that it will continue, perhaps at an even more accelerated pace.

In a secular age, the choice—if, indeed, it is a deliberate decision—not to go to Mass on Sunday makes perfect sense. There are plenty of other things to do on Sunday from sports to shopping to doing laundry to visiting with friends. Church is one option and certainly not as immediately enticing as the others. Besides, God doesn't take my absence personally. Remember, if there is a god in a secular age, it is an impersonal god, a spin-off of Deism. Finally, the often heard complaint about Mass, "I don't get anything out of it," makes sense in an age characterized by expressive individualism (the ritual is given to me and I didn't make it and so it's not mine) and the supreme value of personal choice (I decide what I want to do, and imposing rules is ridiculous).

The fact of declining participation in Sunday Mass now and into the future could be construed in our secular age as a marketing problem. "How do we increase our market share on Sunday mornings?" someone might ask. In fact, some of the Protestant megachurches, notably Willow Creek, have utilized market research to determine how to bring more people into church. The research checks out preferences for parking, seat size, musical styles, child care, length of service, and other things as well. In a Catholic context, however, the challenge is not about upping numbers. Sunday worship is about an essence and identity so close to believers that historically it has been worth dying for.

The Eucharist is so inextricably bound to Catholic faith that it is unimaginable to have a Catholic church without having the Eucharist. At the personal level, it is impossible to be Catholic and not be connected to the Eucharist. Words from John Paul II's apostolic letter *Dies Domini* come to mind: "When, during the persecution of

---

[16] Smith, *Young Catholic America*, 54.

Diocletian, their assemblies were banned with the greatest severity, many were courageous enough to defy the imperial decree and accepted death rather than miss the Sunday Eucharist. This was the case of the martyrs of Abitina, in Proconsular Africa, who replied to their accusers: 'Without fear of any kind we have celebrated the Lord's Supper, because it cannot be missed; that is our law'; 'We cannot live without the Lord's Supper' [*Sine dominico non possumus*]."[17]

Emerging young adults signal future directions for participation in the life of the Catholic Church. Some (very few) participate weekly in what church tradition identifies as "the source and summit of the Christian life," the Mass.[18] More participate sporadically. And the overwhelming majority participates infrequently or rarely. It appears that in the future, Sunday mornings will bring relatively small assemblies of believers together to celebrate and enact the central Christian mystery of the death and resurrection of the Lord. This prediction, of course, depends on extrapolating to the future from current trends, especially with the Catholic emerging adult population.

Acceptance of Catholic beliefs and values. Catholic Christianity has an important doctrinal core. Catholic tradition holds that there are decisively important truths of faith that believers are called to embrace and then live out in the course of their daily lives. Historically, to deny the content of faith or to ignore it as irrelevant was tantamount to separating oneself from the community. The word "heresy" itself means a "cutting off" or "separation." Precise adherence to carefully formulated doctrine, however, runs counter to central tenets of our secular age. Truth, for example, in a pluralistic world does not have the fixed and stable value that it might once have had. It may be truth for me or truth for you, but it never quite gets to the point of being truth in itself, plain and simple, and that includes religious truth. If Catholic emerging adults are more shaped by the secular culture within which they live than the received truth of the Catholic tradition, then one can predict where they stand on elements of Catholic faith does not resemble Catholic belief in any

---

[17] John Paul II, *Dies Domini* (On Keeping the Lord's Day Holy) 46, May 31, 1998.

[18] *Lumen Gentium* 11; see also *Sacrosanctum Concilium* (The Constitution on the Sacred Liturgy) 10.

recognizable way. And Christian Smith's study bears this out for a large swath of young Catholic emerging adults.

An important clarification is in order. The truths expressed and embraced by Catholic faith are not simply cognitive statements of beliefs that belong peculiarly to the Catholic tradition. These truths are truths meant to bring people into relationship with Jesus Christ and to shape the way they live. They are also truths that one can and sometimes ought to die for, as the two-thousand-year history of countless martyrs testifies. So, if Christian Smith's results indicate that Catholic emerging adults have a rather cavalier attitude toward matters of faith, this is a significant issue of basic identity. Such an attitude may stem from the bias of a secular age in the direction of relativism—nothing matters very much and certainly nothing matters absolutely.

Another, even more significant, source for this listless attitude in matters of faith is a lack of exposure to the Catholic faith tradition. This means that these young people may never have learned what the faith tradition is, or if they acquired some knowledge of it, it came by way of popular media, a notoriously unreliable resource for matters concerning Catholic faith. Smith's research does not take him into the specific area of the lack of religious formation of young people, but he does offer a startling statistic that hints at its huge absence: "71 percent of white Catholics report never reading the Bible, while 54 to 60 percent of Hispanic Catholics report the same."[19] If there is no contact ("never read") with the word of God contained in the Scriptures, surely there is bound to be a deficit in knowing what the Catholic faith is about and what its core beliefs and convictions are.

So what exactly do these Catholic emerging adults hold as their beliefs and what does this portend for the future of the Catholic Church? I would select three areas for which Smith offers data, and I will restrict the results to those pertaining to white Catholics. By the third generation, Hispanics are nearly indistinguishable from their white coreligionists. The three areas are (1) view of God; (2) view of Jesus; (3) who goes to heaven.

[19] Smith, *Young Catholic America*, 73.

For their view of God, 54 percent of these young believers hold that God is a personal being involved in the lives of people. Another 38 percent have a "something else" view of God, perhaps as "higher power" or an impersonal force. Finally about 8 percent do not believe in God. Nearly half of the respondents do not have an orthodox belief in God.

The way that Catholic emerging adults view Jesus aligns somewhat more closely with orthodox Catholic teaching: 61 percent believe that he is the Son of God and that he was raised from the dead. At the same time, about 31 percent do not accept him as the Son of God. And approximately 8 percent are unsure about what they believe concerning Jesus. Although 61 percent share belief in Jesus Christ as the Catholic Church teaches it, a relatively large percentage remain unconvinced about the one who is at the center of Christian faith.

The next area raises the question, who goes to heaven? This question represents far more than an invitation to offer a detached opinion. It has a direct bearing on how people view salvation in Jesus Christ, how they respond to it, and what the implications of faith are for living life right now. A stunning 48 percent are either unsure about heaven or simply do not believe in it. Then 24 percent believe that good people or all people go to heaven. Finally, a scant 28 percent have an orthodox belief that those people go to heaven whose sins are forgiven through faith in Jesus Christ.

The Catholic tradition holds that what a person believes is decisively important. As we look to Catholic emerging young adults and project their faith into the future, the content of belief does not seem—in their estimation and practice—to be that important. An important link to Catholic tradition, the convictions of faith, seems likely to weaken as we move into the future.

Were these questions of faith exclusively about articulating and embracing traditional or orthodox formulations of belief, we would already have considerable reason to be concerned. There is, however, another dimension that should dramatically heighten that concern about the future. It is the question of values and putting the convictions of faith into practice in daily life, in other words, the moral implications and consequences of embracing Christian faith. Smith synthesizes the state of the question for Catholic emerging young adults by reflecting on those whom he has been interviewing across their teen years and, now, into emerging young adulthood. It is worthwhile to cite one of his synthetic paragraphs in its entirety:

> Many emerging adults pursue (what they think might be) happiness through experimentation—by "trying out" and "trying on" different identities, careers, relationships, and intoxicating substances. Both the traditions of the Catholic faith generally and its prohibitions against unmarried sex, heavy drinking, and illegal drugs specifically are completely at odds with what it means in this culture to "come of age" as a mature or fulfilled emerging adult, as our interviewees see it. A basic incongruence exists between the central assumptions and values of emerging adult culture and those of the Catholic Church. Many of the teenagers we interviewed in our first wave of data collection agreed with the Church's teaching against sex outside of marriage; but five years later, by wave three, when they had entered emerging adulthood, almost none still held this view and only one or two of those we interviewed actually followed it for religious reasons.[20]

This subsection began with the title "acceptance of Catholic beliefs and values." Our purpose was to see, with the help of Christian Smith's longitudinal sociological study, where Catholic emerging adults stood with Catholic beliefs and values. Smith's study tells us that a very large swath of these Catholic emerging adults is, in effect, unmoored from the Catholic tradition. They may not know it or, if they do know it, they may not understand it. The majority certainly does not accept traditional or orthodox Catholic belief from which they seem largely disconnected or, minimally, to which they are very lightly connected. If this cohort is a leading edge of the church's future, then there is considerable reason to be concerned about the future. Currently, these trends seem to be firmly in place, and any change or reversal seems unlikely. There remains a third and final area to explore, the question of identification and affiliation with the Catholic faith.

[20] Ibid., 118.

General patterns of identification and affiliation with the Catholic faith and the Catholic Church. If we want a sense of the future of the church, then one obvious question needs to be answered: How many young people do we seem to be able to retain now and, so, how many do we anticipate retaining in the future? The question of retention is not just a matter of "hanging on" to individuals. Rather, it means knowing how they identify themselves and how they affiliate with the Catholic faith and the Catholic Church. Understanding these patterns ought to give us some insight into the future. There is, however, a significant difficulty in making these determinations, as Christian Smith discovered in the course of his research.

Smith raises this question: "Who, when it comes to social science analysis of emerging adults, actually *is* a Catholic? The answer may seem simple: people who say they are Catholic. But answering this surprisingly complicated question is actually not so easy. . . . This question does not have a straightforward answer. American youth today often experience unusual life situations that complicate the way they understand and express their religious affiliation(s) and identity(ies)."[21] We cannot and we need not rehearse Smith's carefully argued approach to identifying who actually is a Catholic. He concludes with seven types of Catholics: completely Catholic, mostly Catholic, somewhat Catholic, nominally Catholic, family Catholic, previous Catholic, and secondary Catholic. These types reflect something of the secular culture with its relativistic bent and with postmodernism that refuses to buckle under rigid categories, for example, the dichotomous choice of Catholic or non-Catholic. From all this, I conclude that we must move cautiously and critically when sociological studies suggest overall trends for "the Catholic population." We might never be exactly sure who is included.

For trends of Catholic youth identifying and affiliating as Catholics, I find another result of Smith's research more compelling and helpful. He draws on the narrative accounts of forty-one young people from the beginning of the study when some of them were as young as thirteen years old. In the third wave of investigation and interviews,

---

[21] Ibid., 126.

they are now between eighteen and twenty-three. He is quick to point out that where they stand vis-à-vis Catholicism in not necessarily indicative of where all other emerging adults are who have or have had a connection with the Catholic faith. With that caution and limitation, I think what he uncovers in his third wave of interviews can serve to give us a sketch, if not a precisely detailed portrait, of young Catholics past, present, and perhaps future.

Smith begins with forty-one young people who belonged to the first and second waves of interviews. At this point, with the third wave, where do they now stand? Here is a quick summary of results in Smith's categories. I confess that I found the results startling. Of the forty-one, there are seven apostates who have fully abandoned their Catholic identity and not embraced another. Five are switchers, who have replaced their Catholic identity with an evangelical one. There are another eleven estranged, that is, who hold a Catholic identity but are distanced and critical of the church and unlikely to return. Another six are nominal, that is, nonpracticing but might return. And twelve are engaged, who practice in some way but do not grasp or necessarily fully agree with the Catholic faith. Finally, zero can be categorized as devout, those who practice consistently and both believe and understand the church's teaching.

Again, note that this is a very particular sample. Smith relates that on his own campus, Notre Dame, there are good numbers of devout young Catholics. Obviously, that is more than zero. Still, it would seem when you put this sampling together with some of the more general data from Putnam and Campbell, there is a downward trend and a low retention rate. The numbers are troubling for those of us who care for young people and for the future of the church.

Conclusions and Reflections

We began with a question: What can we expect? In the United States, what can we expect for the future of the Catholic Church and for the future of believers? The short answer, based on the philosophical, historical, cultural, and sociological studies we have considered, is decline. We can anticipate such a decline because of trends that have long been in motion.

We live, in the words of Charles Taylor, in a secular age. Both Taylor and James Davison Hunter help us see that over a long period a kind of secularity has shaped the culture in which we live. In fact, the forces of secularity have shaped our culture and our very selves far beyond anything believers could do to shape secularity itself. Furthermore, a closed-ended form of secularity has been ascendant and gives no sign of retreating. Religious commentators correctly see secularity moving toward increasing tension with the traditions of faith and perhaps arriving at a point of complete incompatibility with the claims and practices of faith. In stark contrast to secularity, Christian faith seems antihuman and even irrational.

Once, the church managed the means of communication and the arts. Now, the "rich producers" of culture in communications, the arts, and education are thoroughly secular. And the secular perspective shapes the ongoing human narrative—telling us who we are and what our purpose is—something previously reserved for religious traditions. A closed-ended secular perspective also uses technology and drives economies forward devoid of values and is guided only by the principle "if it can be done, do it." Pope Francis identifies this state of affairs with the emergence of a new and ruthless idolatry. It is "the idolatry of money and the dictatorship of an impersonal economy lacking a truly human purpose. The worldwide crisis affecting finance and the economy lays bare their imbalances and, above all, their lack of real concern for human beings; man is reduced to one of his needs alone: consumption."[22] Pope Francis effectively uncovers the failed humanism of closed-ended secularization.

Even in a nation of believers—as the United States is by any standards—the forces of secularity dominate in shaping the culture, so that believers often feel like strangers in their own land. And closed-ended secularity delivers a complex set of messages to "religious America." Sometimes, secularity actually prizes forms of religiosity but only as interesting and collectible artifacts. Some of the most ardent supporters of Christian art and music, for example, have no interest in what inspired the art or music but rather invest in their

---

[22] Pope Francis, *Evangelii Gaudium* (The Joy of the Gospel) 55, November 24, 2013.

aesthetic values. Another strategy of closed-ended secularity vis-à-vis religiosity is to erase faith's imprint in society (politics, law, institutional life) to the extent that religiosity seems to create roadblocks to full human emancipation, that is, the full and free self-determination of individuals. In recent decades, this has been noticeably evident in the collisions of religion and feminism and religion and gay rights. A final strategy of closed-ended secularism is to contain religiosity, that is, to enclose it and relegate it to a private and personal practice, so that it cannot contaminate the public sphere with its prejudices and various forms of human diminishment.

We have been considering a closed-ended form of secularity, and that form inevitably finds itself at loggerheads with religion and faith. It is not, however, the only possible form of secularity. It is also possible, as the Second Vatican Council affirmed and as we already noted, to have an open-ended secularity that fosters and continues the good developments that have emerged from secularization but not at a cost of diminishing or eliminating religion or faith. In fact, faith and religion can flourish in a particular kind of secular environment. What might that environment look like?

Open-ended secularity shares with other forms of secularity a commitment to rationality, to human reason, and to an empirical-logical knowledge process. Unlike a closed-ended form of secularity, an open-ended form also embraces other forms of knowledge that are not irrational but suprarational and intuitive. In a way reminiscent of Kurt Gödel's incompleteness theorem, an open-ended secularity recognizes the incompleteness of any system closed in on itself. This form of secularity also emphasizes human solidarity and relational and participatory priorities in the social, political, and economic organization of human beings. This stands in stark contrast to a closed-ended form of secularity that asserts and affirms a radical autonomy of the individual. Finally, this open-ended secularity allows a place for transcendent hope, the possibility of a future that is not merely dependent on human construction.

We are most familiar with closed-ended forms of secularity. And they suggest a future of religion and faith in decline. In that context, the church can be thrust into a defensive mode and even a struggle for survival, which happened in the totalitarian regimes in the twentieth century. Although the closed-ended forms of secularity seem likely to dominate the future, because they dominate the current cultural landscape in America, an alternate future scenario could emerge. An open-ended secularity that fits more comfortably with religion and faith commitments remains a possibility but, in truth, a less likely one.

In light of life in a secular age, we asked a specific question: How does the secular culture affect young people whose religious commitments today give us a window into the future of faith and the church in the United States? Sociological studies, primarily those conducted by Christian Smith, indicated the powerful shaping force of the secular culture. For example, the secular culture has formed large numbers of young people—perhaps not all and perhaps not all with the same force—in certain dispositions: attention to the here and now, a focus on the individual, the primacy of personal choice, a desire for personal expression, a contentment with short-term results and realities, and a diminished sense or even lack of what Paul Tillich called "ultimate concern." These dispositions have a dramatic impact on faith and religious participation. They translate into weak communal participation in rituals including the core ritual of Sunday Mass, loose doctrinal adherence, a marginal impact of faith on daily life choices, and a relative absence of the tangible faith symbols that serve as identity markers and reminders of transcendent meaning. For the future, it looks like much fewer "real Catholics" (even as Christian Smith admittedly struggled to pinpoint the meaning of that category) and many more either very loosely affiliated with the church or simply gone from the community of faith.

Permit me to add a personal anecdotal postscript to explain how that anticipated bleak future for the Catholic faith and the Catholic Church in the United States has already in some measure arrived. In Chicago, they call the obituary notices in the daily newspapers the Irish sports page. The Irish are famously diligent in perusing the notices, finding out who died, and determining the wakes and funerals that they should attend. I've caught some of that Irish spirit, and I generally do check through the obituaries. And I have found some significant indicators for the life of faith and the life of the church.

More and more I see names in the obituaries that have a Catholic ring to them—Irish, Italian, and Polish, for example—but there is no indication that a funeral Mass will be celebrated. For whatever reason, what is a deeply ingrained Catholic practice—the funeral Mass—is bypassed in favor of a service at the funeral home. And then there are other obituaries that do mention a Catholic church service, but it is listed as a "celebration of life."

How people deal with death is an accurate barometer of their faith and their participation in the life of the church. The experience of death puts us squarely before the fundamental questions of our existence. Does death have the last word? If so, then it makes sense to memorialize, to eulogize, and to celebrate the life of the deceased, because that is all that is left to us. Does the death and resurrection of the Lord made present in the celebration of the Mass not really matter that much? If so, then it makes sense to bypass the funeral Mass and the opportunity to reaffirm our faith that in dying Christ destroyed our death and in his rising restored our life. Clearly our funeral practices do provide a barometer of faith. What we do with death—certainly in a Christian context—puts us in touch with our faith or lack of faith.

These are my impressions from a casual reading of the obituaries in the Chicago newspapers. In fact, I have found confirmation from priests in parishes and from some statistical data as well. Catholic funerals traditionally celebrated are on the decline. That fact illustrates that Catholic faith and participation are not only on a downward slope among Catholic emerging adults but, in some measure, a decline in faith has already begun to reach an older, dying generation.

After this, anyone who loves and cares for the church and its people and faith must surely be tempted to profound discouragement. That discouragement would seem to stem from what looks like a future collapse that has already begun. And if all we have is this data from philosophy, history, culture, and sociology, then there is more than sufficient reason for sadness. In fact, there is more to the story. The future is not assured in any particular form. We must leave room for the unexpected. And we will explore that shortly. Besides, we are not just the pawns of forces beyond us. As people of faith, we believe that we can be by God's grace and, indeed, are protagonists of our own history. And that is also something that we shall explore later. Our next step is to consider the unexpected.

2

Is There Anything Unexpected That We Could Possibly Expect?

Trying to map the future is a notoriously difficult enterprise. Fortunes have been lost by entrepreneurs trying to predict what people *will* want, what they *will* need, or what fashion they *will* embrace tomorrow. The case of the failed Ford Edsel from the 1950s is the classic cautionary tale of the perils of prognosticating the automotive future. And it sometimes works in the opposite direction as well. Who before the 1950s could have anticipated the commercial success of the hula hoop, nothing but a circular piece of plastic to encourage gyrations that amounted to meaningless motion?

As much as we try and as much as we employ what means we have available, we can never claim pinpoint accuracy in predicting the future, whether that is the future of a commercial enterprise or the future of the Catholic Church in the United States. Surprises lurk around the corner. The unanticipated can be as much a part of our future as our most carefully calibrated projections.

In response to our first question—what can we expect?—we utilized the means we have available to project into the future of Catholic faith and Catholic Church life in America. The means included history, philosophy, cultural analysis, and sociological studies. The results suggested a rather bleak picture for the future, a future of decline in religious participation and adherence to faith based on the projection of current trends and the prevailing secular Zeitgeist. That portrait of the future is not, however, our inevitable future. I already noted that a spiritually healthy open-ended secularity could be an alternative to the currently dominant closed-ended secularity that diminishes religion and faith, although many factors today suggest that it would be an unlikely alternative. Still, there are other unexpected elements that could alter what seems to be a future of religious and spiritual decline. And in this chapter, we will consider some of these unexpected elements, possible and unanticipated twists and turns of our future.

Unexpected Saints

As the church passes through the vicissitudes of history, the Spirit of God accompanies the church on its pilgrimage home to God. At various points, because of God's providential care for his people, the Spirit raises up men and women as outstanding models and instruments of the holiness of God. They give new shape to the church and enable it to stay faithful to the Lord. Here is how the Second Vatican Council describes this reality of the saints in our midst: "God shows to men [and women], in a vivid way, his presence and his face in the lives of those companions of ours in the human condition who are more perfectly transformed into the image of Christ. . . . He speaks to us in them and offers us a sign of this kingdom, to which we are powerfully attracted, so great a cloud of witnesses is there given . . . and such a witness to the truth of the Gospel" (*Lumen Gentium* 50).

The raising up of saints to encourage and shape the life of the church is not something that we can program. In surprising and unexpected ways, the Spirit of God raises up men and women who change the church to make it conform more closely to the Lord. Historically, in completely unanticipated ways, the saints have been present to the church in situations of threat or spiritual tepidness or new and formidable challenges. They not only inspire and encourage, but they also give some structure and creative direction to new initiatives. Consider the following examples.

Some five hundred years into the Christian era, the social and civic structures of the Roman Empire were unraveling, the vast migrations of those called "barbarians" increased, and the number of those in need of evangelization expanded greatly. The general instability of this period hampered the Christian mission and the life of the church generally. In this situation, God raised up the great saint Benedict of Nursia (d. ca. 547 AD). By founding monasteries in Italy and writing what has become known as the Rule of St. Benedict, he is credited with being the founder of Western monasticism. In a period of upheaval and instability, he provided the structure for stable communities that became a point of reference for church life throughout Europe. These monastery communities also became a vehicle to carry on the mission of evangelization for both the old and new populations of Europe. Benedict's influence shaped the church and the faith lives of countless Christians in challenging historical moments. His presence and his impact could not have been anticipated. Benedict represented an unexpected grace in a critical time.

The church in the time of Francis of Assisi (d. 1226 AD) found itself in a situation much different than that of Benedict. In the thirteenth century, the church enjoyed an established status and a measure of material well-being. And yet, the church also seemed to lack fervor and seemed far from the freshness of the Gospel. A kind of complacency had crept into the church that made religious practices routine, faith blunted in its passion, and religious commitments often shallow. The Spirit then raised up Francis. The Spirit first lifted him up from the numbing complacencies of bourgeois existence. At the church of San Damiano, Francis encountered the living Christ and, in that encounter, discovered the power of the Gospel. Closeness of the incarnate Word of God as the crucified one became the hallmark of Francis's preaching. It also shaped a lifestyle of simplicity and care for the poor and marginalized. It is no exaggeration to say that Francis revivified the church by recentering the focus of Christians on Christ and by summoning them to let their relationship with Christ shape their daily lives. In all of this, we perceive Francis as an unexpected presence in a relatively "successful" but complacent church. In a most remarkable way, this ragged figure led the church into an unanticipated future.

A final example of an unexpected saint raised up by God to lead the church into an unanticipated future lived closer to our own time. She is Thérèse of Lisieux (d. 1897). The life of Thérèse was a short twenty-four years and all of those lived in obscurity. She did not leave an extensive set of writings, simply an account of her life and some correspondence. For all these limitations, she is a pivotal figure who brought the church into an entirely renewed sense of spirituality that would correspond to needs of the century that would follow her and into our own epoch. Without exaggeration, we can say that she revolutionized Christian spirituality. How so? She transformed what had been idealized elitist forms of spirituality with a focus on mysticism or extreme asceticism into the accessible and democratic path of her Little Way. And that meant finding God in the ordinary course of life. She also transformed the Jansenistic legacy she inherited with its emphasis on observance of the law into a singular focus on the primacy of love, the love of God and the love of neighbor. Finally, as she experienced her own form of the dark night of faith at the end of her life, she articulated a dimension of spirituality that would prove crucial for the twentieth century, marked as it was by bloodshed and destruction. That dimension was discovering God's presence in what seemed to be the felt absence of God. And that discovery was enabled through complete trust and surrender.

These examples show us how God has acted to lead the church into the future in particular and decisive moments of history. When the church faced an unstable world (Benedict) or when the church itself suffered from a stultifying complacency (Francis) or when the spiritual energies of the church seemed insufficient to meet the modern world (Thérèse), God led the church into the future by raising up men and women who sparked the imagination of believers and opened new paths of renewal. What, then, are the lessons for us today?

Obviously, we cannot engineer the work of the Holy Spirit in raising up saints for our time. That must be left to God's good grace. For our part, we can watch and wait. We can stay open and attentive to the action of God in our brothers and sisters. Some say that in this moment God has raised up Pope Francis as a person who can ignite the imagination of believers as they grapple with an uncertain future. That may be so, but it may also take some time to understand if that, indeed, is the case and do so with greater precision. In the meanwhile, God entrusts us with the task of confident waiting. We wait for his action, knowing that he is faithful to his people. When a shadow seems to fall over our lives and the church and the future is full of uncertainty, then he surprises us in ways that we could never have anticipated. He works in and through individuals and enables them to be vehicles or instruments of renewal. This is the first unexpected thing that we could expect.

An Unexpectedly Robust Church, but Maybe for the Wrong Reasons

Unexpectedly, the church can become a robust player in the social and political order. This can happen as a reaction to what seems to be a decline of religious faith and its influence in a secular environment. For example, Pew Research featured a summary of research with this paradoxical title: "Public Sees Religion's Influence Waning: Growing Appetite for Religion in Politics."[1] Because nearly three-quarters of the public thinks that religion is losing its influence in American life, it seems that "a growing share of the American public [49 percent] wants religion to play a greater and more pronounced role in U.S. politics." With growing secularity, it is counterintuitive that the public wants more religious influence and specifically in the political arena. Is this a harbinger of an unexpectedly robust situation for the church and for faith? Probably not, although it is not entirely out of the realm.

Sometimes given social and historical factors—and not necessarily authentically spiritual movements—can give rise to a favorable situation for the church. In such a situation, the church is well advised to remain cautious. The relationship between the Catholic Church and the French political movement known as Action Française (AF) in the first half of the twentieth century underscores this need for caution. AF's ideological architect was Charles Maurras. Although an agnostic, he supported the establishment of Catholicism as the state religion of France as part of a larger monarchist and nationalist agenda. His promotion of Catholicism was purely utilitarian,

---

[1] Pew Research Center, "Public Sees Religion's Influence Waning: Growing Appetite for Religion in Politics," September 22, 2014, http://www.pewforum.org/2014/09/22/public-sees-religions-influence-waning-2/.

because he envisioned a shared religion as an essential element of social cohesion. Maurras's position supported and encouraged the participation of conservative French Catholics in AF. Eventually, the defective and corrupting elements of the ideology behind AF led Pius XI to condemn it in 1926, although the condemnation was later lifted in the face of a communist threat in France. Catholic thinkers addressed the tangle of religious and political themes. For example, a great Catholic philosopher of the twentieth century, Jacques Maritain—to remain faithful to his Catholic faith—pulled back from both the right and left in his well-known essay "A Letter on Independence."[2] The AF movement fizzled, but it was reincarnated in various political parties that exist even today. One can easily read the current situation of tension in France with its mainly Muslim immigrant communities as a potential motivation for a resurgence of Catholic identity. Will that happen? No one knows for sure. The point is that—unexpectedly—political and social situations can give at least a veneer of robustness to faith, church, and religion.

Our study of history, philosophy, culture, and sociology suggests probable directions for the role of the church, faith, and religion in the future. And from our conclusions we understand that those directions indicate decline. But these projections always remain probable, never entirely certain. A confluence of social and political forces can seem to create and sustain a robust church that exercises influence. Such things happen not as foregone conclusions but always in the range of some possibility.

An Unexpected Disenchantment with Secularity

As both Charles Taylor and James Davison Hunter describe it, a closed-in form of secularity dominates our culture in North America and much of Europe as well. Neither Taylor nor Hunter expect that secularity will loosen its grip on everyday life. More significantly for our concerns, in their estimation, secular values and directions will

---

[2] Jacques Maritain, *Integral Humanism, Freedom in the Modern World, and A Letter on Independence*, trans. O. Bird, J. Evans, and R. O'Sullivan (Notre Dame, IN: University of Notre Dame Press, 1996), 121–39.

inevitably be antithetical to the outlooks of faith and religion. But is this inevitable secularity that is inevitably antithetical to faith and religion a cinched thing? Could there be some unexpected chinks in the armor of secularity? And could this lead to a renewed "legitimation" of faith and religion in public life?

Jürgen Habermas and Thomas Nagel are two philosophers who both retain an atheist or agnostic identity, at least for their philosophical methodological purposes. And yet, as they come from two different perspectives, respectively of social philosophy and evolutionary theory, they both suggest that a closed-ended secularity may be insufficient to explain and to deal with the human condition.

Habermas engaged in a colloquium with philosophers from the Jesuit School of Philosophy in Munich. His lead presentation is evocatively titled "An Awareness of What is Missing."[3] The beginning of that essay captures Habermas's intuition about a particular cultural lack in a secular and post-secular age:

> On April 9, 1991, a memorial service for Max Frisch was held in St. Peter's Church in Zürich. It began with Karin Pilliod, Frisch's partner, reading out a brief declaration written by the deceased. It stated, among other things: "We let our nearest speak, and without an 'amen.' I am grateful to the ministers of St. Peter's in Zürich . . . for their permission to place the coffin in the church during our memorial service. The ashes will be strewn somewhere." Two friends spoke. No priest, no blessing. The mourners were made up of intellectuals, most of whom had little time for church and religion. Frisch himself had drawn up the menu for the meal that followed. At the time the ceremony did not strike me as peculiar. However, its form, place and progression *were* peculiar. Clearly, Max Frisch, an agnostic who rejected any profession of faith, had sensed the awkwardness of non-religious burial practices and, by his choice of place, publicly declared that the enlightened modern age has failed to find a suitable replacement for a religious way of coping with the final *rîte de passage* which brings life to a close.

---

[3] Jürgen Habermas et al., *An Awareness of What is Missing: Faith and Reason in a Post-Secular Age*, trans. C. Cronin (Malden, MA: Polity Press, 2010), 19–23.

One can interpret this gesture as an expression of melancholy over something which has been irretrievably lost. Yet one can also view the ceremony as a paradoxical event which tells us something about secular reason, namely that it is unsettled by the opaqueness of its merely apparently clarified relations to religion.[4]

Habermas's account of Max Frisch's funeral points to "what is missing." Initially, what seems to be missing is a ritual to express or deal with the especially significant moment of death. That ritual absence, however, speaks to another, deeper deficit. Habermas implies that secularity seems incapable of fully expressing the full range of human experience, which includes death as a singularly important component. For whatever reason, the secular approach remains insufficient, awkward, and inadequate to name and address the human experience of death. Perhaps, I can take it a step further.

Habermas does not directly suggest that secularity is insufficient in its capacity to express what is human. I draw that implication from his observations. I see clearly that the self-contained humanism of secularity is a purely immanent reality. Because this form of humanism has no reference point beyond itself, it cannot situate human death in any other, larger, and meaningful horizon. After all, death signifies the end of human life. The manifest irony of humanistic secularity facing human death is that it cannot fully account for humanity in the context of this particular and profound human experience, because there is no larger framework within which this experience can be situated. From my perspective, it looks like a chink in the armor of secularity begins to appear.

Later in another essay, Habermas addresses the social and political challenges that we face on a global level. Ever since 9/11 we have tried to organize ourselves to achieve the political regulation of a multicultural world society. We can try to do that on the basis of a rational morality, but our secular environment established us in a universe of individual claims and individual duties. We may, he suggests, have the cognitive moral insight for individuals, but this

---

[4] Ibid., 15–16.

"does not foster any impulse towards solidarity, that is, towards morally guided, collective action." He then elaborates on this point: "Secular morality is not inherently embedded in communal practices. Religious consciousness, by contrast, preserves an essential connection to the ongoing practice of life within a community and, in the case of the major world religions, to the observances of united global communities of all of the faithful. The religious consciousness of the individual can derive stronger impulses towards action in solidarity, even from a purely moral point of view, from this universalistic communitarianism."[5]

Again, Habermas does not directly assert that secular humanism is intrinsically incapable of bringing human partners together for collective moral action, which is the only effective action for the transformation of the social order. I do think that implication can be drawn from his observations. Secular humanism without another reference point beyond itself cannot provide the possibility of moral cohesion that would be the basis for collective moral action. It is, in other words, insufficient to have shared individual moral convictions. It is crucial to have a shared commitment, a community of life or communion, and solidarity in committed action. Historically, these elements of commitment, communion, and solidarity have rested on shared religious or faith commitment and common participation in a way of life.

Habermas does not count himself among believers. At the same time, he honestly identifies what his fellow secular commentators seem to assiduously avoid—an awareness of what is missing in the secular worldview.

Thomas Nagel, a noted American philosopher, also identifies what is missing but from a much different perspective. He steadfastly maintains his identity as an atheist but affirms the inadequacy of a purely materialist account of the world, an account that is the stock in trade for secular thinking today. The scientific-physical explanation, he asserts, is reductive and inadequate. It is doubtful, he says, that "the reality of such features of our world as consciousness, intentionality, meaning, purpose, thought, and value can be accommodated in a universe consisting at the most basic level only of physical facts—facts, however sophisticated, of the kind revealed by the physical sciences."[6]

As Nagel asserts the inadequacy of materialism to offer a comprehensive account of our world, especially the world of consciousness, he is also convinced of the inadequacy of theism. Still, it seems to me, he reveals another chink in the armor of a secularity governed by an exclusively materialist worldview. And that chink has to do with teleology or purpose in the world and, of course by extension, in our lives. He describes what an adequate account might look like:

> The essential character of such an understanding would be to explain the appearance of life, consciousness, reason, and knowledge neither as accidental side effects of the physical laws of nature nor as the result of intentional intervention in nature from without [theism] but as an unsurprising if not inevitable consequence of the order that governs the natural world from within. That order would have to include physical law, but if life is not just a physical phenomenon, the origin and evolution of life and mind will not be explainable by physics and chemistry alone. An expanded, but still unified, form of explanation will be needed, and I suspect it will have to include teleological elements.[7]

And later, after enumerating various elements that a "theory of everything" has to explain, he includes at the end "the development of consciousness into an instrument of transcendence that can grasp objective reality and objective value."[8]

Despite his avowed atheism, when Nagel ventures to suggest that adequate explanations of our world must include internally coherent purpose and objectivity in perception and value, he seems to me to flirt dangerously with religious faith. This fact has not escaped the

---

[6] Thomas Nagel, *Mind and Cosmos: Why the Materialist Neo-Darwinian Conception of Nature is Almost Certainly False* (New York: Oxford University Press, 2012), 13.

[7] Ibid., 32.

[8] Ibid., 85.

notice of his scientific and philosophical colleagues who have been largely dismissive of his position without offering, in my estimation, adequate counterarguments.

What are we to make of these reflections from Habermas and Nagel? The title of this section reads "an unexpected disenchantment with secularity." The title both underreports the current climate and, at the same time, overstates a possible future outcome. In the current climate, as the so-called culture wars manifest, plenty of people are *already* disenchanted with secularity. In fact, they were never enchanted by it. At the same time, they do not belong to the earlier identified class of "rich producers of culture." They are, therefore, unable to shift the culture in another, "more Christian" direction, as they might wish despite their significant numbers. The title of this section also overstates a possible future outcome. Clearly, both Habermas and Nagel have not surrendered their secular convictions for religious faith. What they reveal is the inadequacy of secularity as a total and comprehensive system, especially in its closed-ended form. As the title of Habermas's essay simply but effectively states, there is an awareness of something missing. Similarly, Nagel's contention isn't to propose a Creator to explain the universe but rather to show the inadequacy of a materialist-reductionist vision of that universe. Their thinking reveals chinks in the armor of secularity, but it hardly presages its demise. Still, they do belong to that class of the rich producers of culture, and the qualifications of secularity that they assert do serve to diminish the absolute hold that has dominated the secular mindset. And so, with the intimations that Habermas and Nagel offer, a future and unexpected turn could be some openness to faith and religion *in* a qualified and more open form of secularity. That result could have enormous significance for the future of faith, religion, and church.

Conclusion: What Can We Expect?

After we examine the historical, philosophical, cultural, and sociological trajectory of religious faith and the church, we can clearly see a future that belongs to what Charles Taylor calls a secular age. That is not a bad thing in itself. There are positive benefits. One of

Taylor's important lead questions was, "Why was it virtually impossible not to believe in God in, say, 1500 in our Western society, while in 2000 many of us find this not only easy, but even inescapable?"[9] The framing of the question means that faith in a secular age is not simply a part of an inherited cultural package ("virtually impossible not to believe in God"), but faith must necessarily be intentional, deliberate, and free. Those characteristics signal authentic faith, as the Christian tradition has understood it.

When we hear James Davison Hunter speak about the position of faith in this secular culture, he seems to suggest something that is, at least, initially troubling for believers. That is, faith may matter very much to us who believe, but it doesn't matter very much to the world in which we live. A triumphalist Christian faith finds this a difficult pill to swallow. On the other hand, the very hiddenness of faith and its undetectable effects in the world clearly resonate with the teachings of Jesus, who told his followers that they would be like salt, leaven, and even very small seeds in the world.

The sociological studies of Christian Smith and others suggest the next generation, our future demographic, will shrink the population of the church in America. There are fewer numbers now, and it seems even fewer in the future. That suggests a uniformly bleak future for the church. Embedded, however, in the pattern described by Smith that forms a part of his book's subtitle—"in, out of, and gone from the church"—is a surprising fact that Smith reveals and that colors and qualifies the bleakness. The next generation does not so much deliberately leave faith, religion, and church as drift away from realities that they have never really known. They don't decide, they meander without much information or formation. For whatever reason, an older generation has failed to communicate with them and support the meaning and possibility of faith and religious participation. They are not deliberately "lost," and certainly not irretrievably so.

Our quick survey of unexpected possibilities yields its own results and offers some hope. In the past, God has unexpectedly raised up

---

[9] Taylor, *A Secular Age*, 25.

saints to meet the needs of a given generation. That fact encourages our watchfulness and our hope in our own historical moment. We also know from history that religion and politics can fuse in a way that gives religion an unexpected ascendancy. History also instructs us to be cautious about religious revivals based on political expediency. In those cases, authentic religious faith can suffer. Finally, even thoroughgoing convinced secularists, such as Habermas and Nagel, are aware of secularity's insufficiency as a comprehensive and closed system of thinking and living. With that assessment, a door edges open to possibilities of faith and religion flourishing in a more modestly aligned secularity.

What, then, can we expect? Certainly, not a precise and detailed portrait of the future of culture and the future of faith and religion and church within that culture. Some parameters are clear. For example, secularity is not about to vanish, and it would probably not be to faith and religion's advantage were that to happen. Secondly, there are seeds of hope for faith, religion, and church to flourish. Finally, everything that we have considered to this point indicates that we ought not to succumb to strategic paralysis. As people of faith, we can move forward, we can develop ways to bring faith to a world in need, and we can offer—even in a secular age—what no one else can offer, a reason for hope.

These conclusions lead us to take up the question of the next chapter of this book—what can we do? What are the options available to us?

3

What Can We Do?

First, a Question: Who Are "We"?

Before identifying what can be done (passive voice), I want to identify who can do it (active voice). This is the question of agency, and it is also the question of the audience that I have been addressing in these reflections. Let me explain this in greater detail.

In the first part of my reflections, I raised questions and concerns about the future of the Catholic faith, religion, and church in the United States. I did not do this alone but rather with the help of a wide spectrum of experts in philosophy, history, cultural studies, and sociology. Obviously, my purpose was not just to lay out problems and challenges. I very much want to map, at least initially, our responses to the current and anticipated situation of the Catholic Church in our nation. That means that I need to identify some directions for the future. I need to respond to the question, where do we go? First, however, I must answer other questions: Who goes? Who acts? Who engages the challenges ahead of us?

In chapter 1, I said that *we* are the protagonists or actors in our own history and in our own communities. Those of us who stand in the community of faith and who believe do have a collective sense of ourselves that is a shared identity and a shared commitment in faith. Presumably, because you are reading and following these reflections, you are interested and invested in the future of the church. With me, you want to know what *I* can do, what *we* can do. In this author-reader alliance of common interest and concern, we share an understanding of the need to do something. Even more, we may actually be willing to assume responsibility and be agents who act. Our agency, how we act, however, is not a simple matter. As people of faith, we belong to the church, which exists in this world in several dimensions, each one of which shapes how we can and ought to act on the church's behalf.

Let me briefly explain these different dimensions of the church's existence and how they can affect our involvement in the church's future. I draw inspiration from a book by Jean-Paul Audet, *The Gospel Project*.[1] Audet was the world's foremost scholar of the *Didachê*, which, after the New Testament, is one of the earliest documents of the Christian tradition. He uses his background to retrieve a sense of the church from the gospels and the writings of the apostolic age. Audet, as I read him, identifies three essential dimensions of the church's existence: as an organization, as a community, and as a movement. How we act for and on behalf of the church as it moves into the future depends very much on this three-dimensional framework of the church.

The Church as Organization

The church is an organization or a visibly structured institution with clear positions of institutional leadership, such as the pope, bishops, priests, deacons, and an assortment of other church professionals. This leadership is both necessary and helpful, and its roots are in the Gospel. It also comes with a cost. Historically, it has fostered a tendency among Catholics at large to defer to that leadership and become passive. Catholics at large would generally not perceive themselves as the active agents of renewal and mission, although that is what we hope for and need. The organizational or institutional life of the church, however, cannot be reduced to its structured leadership. There is far more to the tangible and visible dimension of the church than its leadership. So, for example, Pope Francis envisions a

---

[1] Jean-Paul Audet, *The Gospel Project*, trans. E. Bonin (New York: Paulist Press, 1969).

much wider organizational participation in evangelization than the narrow band of structured leadership. He writes, "Evangelization is the task of the Church. The Church, as the agent of evangelization, is more than an organic and hierarchical institution; she is first and foremost a people advancing on its pilgrim way towards God. She is certainly a *mystery* rooted in the Trinity, yet she exists concretely in history as a people of pilgrims and evangelizers, transcending any institutional expression, however necessary" (*Evangelii Gaudium* 111). And later, rather starkly, he says, "All the baptized, whatever their position in the Church or their level of instruction in the faith, are agents of evangelization, and it would be insufficient to envisage a plan of evangelization to be carried out by professionals while the rest of the faithful would simply be passive recipients" (ibid. 120).

The agents or actors, therefore, who will do something as we face the concerns and challenges of the future of faith, religion, and church seem to be all who have a stake in faith, not just the specialists. Certainly, in the Catholic tradition, ordained ministers have had and will have a particular role to play in initiating, encouraging, and overseeing what the church does and where it goes. That particular and unique role, however, does not mean that the ordained are the exclusive actors. To the question, "Who are those who can do something?" we can confidently respond, "In the first place, they are all who belong to and form part of the visible organization and institutional life that belongs to the church."

The Church as Community

The church is not only an organization or institution but also a community or communion. From an experiential perspective, that means those in the church have treasured and valued connections and relationships with others in faith. These connections and relationships cut across generational, historical, and geographical boundaries. And, even more significantly, they are not merely horizontal relationships linking us with each other; they are singularly rooted in a grand transcendent or vertical relationship in the mystery of Christ by the power of the Holy Spirit. That is the power of faith to link us to each other and to God in a communion or community.

Once we are aware of the richness of these connections in faith lived in the church, we are mobilized to do something to preserve, foster, and deepen the relationships and the communion.

Again, we raise the question of who can do something to meet the future and the challenges of faith, religion, and church. Now from the perspective of the church as community, we can clearly affirm that the agents are those who have experienced relationships and connections in faith. Their experience of community and communion enables and mobilizes them to do what needs to be done to meet the future.

The Church as Movement

The church is not only an organization and a community, but also a movement. Following the Lord's mandate to go forth into the whole world and to be salt, light, and leaven, the church is a mission and a purpose. The parables of the coming of the reign of God underscore the dynamic nature of the church as the very seed of that reign. Believers then experience within themselves a responsibility that carries them beyond themselves to a waiting world that is so much in need of the Gospel. Pope Francis has spoken often and eloquently of the dynamic, missionary dimension of the church. He cites St. Pope John Paul II in saying, "The Church's closeness to Jesus is part of a common journey; 'communion and mission are profoundly interconnected'" (*Evangelii Gaudium* 23). And later, he draws on the *Aparecida Document* to say forcefully, "Throughout the world, let us be 'permanently in a state of mission'" (ibid. 25).

When we truly understand the church as movement, we also recognize how all of us as believers must contribute to the pilgrimage of God's people. Confronting today's challenges and concerns for faith, religion, and church as we move into an uncharted tomorrow is not an optional exercise for us who believe. That essential and perennial task belongs to everyone who is part of this movement that is the church. We are the ones who can and ought to do something.

Who Are the Agents and Protagonists of the Future?

As we understand the church's three-dimensional existence—as organization, as community, and as movement—we gain clarity in identifying the agents who will or ought to act and do something for the future. The agents are coextensive with those who make up the church as a structured organization or institution, as a community and communion living in a set of connections and relationships, and as a movement that expresses and realizes mission and purpose. Who can do something to meet the future? It emerges clearly that all of us who are part of the church have responsibility, a fact that may surprise us or may make some of us uncomfortable. It is a fact, however, that will not go away.

These reflections on who exactly can or ought to do something may appear to belabor the obvious. In fact, they are very necessary. If anything, we should learn from the fate of so many grand pastoral plans that rest in the graveyard of the best of intentions. The plans may have been quite sound in themselves and theologically well grounded. The problem, which keeps repeating itself, is the lack of ownership and the lack of defined agents to implement the plan. As we look ahead, we now have a better sense of who the protagonists are in meeting the present and future challenges of faith, religion, and church.

What, Then, Can We Do?

There are several options. We can choose to stay on our current course, in effect, to do nothing new. We can decide that we are shrinking and then foster the process that leads to a smaller, leaner, and more committed church. Finally (as discussed in the next chapter), we can act positively and proactively by taking into account all that we have considered in the first part of our reflections and then creating responses that make a difference. It is important that we examine each one of these possibilities in some detail before we decide on a direction.

Do Nothing New

A first option is to do nothing new but to stay on the track that we have been following. In other words, we just keep going until the batteries give out. We continue on with the church as we have been. Initially, many people may judge this choice not only as ill-advised but also as unreasonable. Why would we do nothing, when we are so keenly aware of the challenges that face us as a community of faith?

In fact, although this may not be a good choice, it is not an unreasonable one. There are reasons for staying on the current course. For example, one can survey the "players" and quickly see who they are. The vast majority of people invested in the life of the church are older people, and that goes for church leadership as well. Older people often lack an adventuresome edge that would enable them to forge a new path or take a new direction.

Spirituality can also provide another reason for doing nothing new. If everything is in God's hands, then God will provide. We can question whether this kind of passivity is what God really wants from us. Still, in some quarters, this line of pious reasoning holds sway. It has a spiritual air about it, and it is not new. Jeremiah the prophet, for example, excoriated the passivity of the people who refused to address their crumbling national situation and instead relied on old pieties, such as a misplaced trust in the presence of the temple among them. "Amend your ways and your doings, and let me dwell with you in this place. Do not trust in these deceptive words: 'This is the temple of the LORD, the temple of the LORD, the temple of the LORD'" (Jer 7:3-4).

And yet another reason for doing nothing and staying on the current course of church life has to do with blaming the culture for our problems. It's not our fault, people might say, that faith, religion, and church are in a state of decline. We didn't create the secularism that daily assaults us. We didn't break the dish, and we don't have to pick up the pieces. In fact, this position smacks of the aggrieved victimhood that James Davison Hunter identified. In short, this position says that what is not our problem is not our responsibility.

Others question the value of doing something different, because they anticipate that it won't do any good anyway. The question they raise is, what's the use? And there is some plausibility here. The trajectories from the studies that we have cited argue against the likelihood of changing direction. In that light, it seems better to surrender to the inevitable. This state of mind and soul suggests the defeatism that Pope Francis has declared as a great enemy of pastoral initiatives: "One of the more serious temptations which stifles boldness and zeal is a defeatism which turns us into querulous and disillusioned pessimists" (*Evangelii Gaudium* 85).

There are other reasons for doing nothing different and staying on the same course. It may be a fear that an initiative will backfire and things will get worse. Or, it may be an almost childlike clinging to the security of what is known. Or, it may be the inability to imagine or conceive an alternative.

Staying the course and doing nothing, in my judgment, is a poor choice. In given contexts, however, it is an understandable one. The do-nothing and stay-the-course option also hides risks. First of all, we collectively risk falling under the spell of the psychological mechanism of denial and, like the proverbial ostrich, burying our heads in the sand. We can also risk not hearing and heeding God's call in our situation. And God does, indeed, continue to summon us to engage our circumstances and not simply to hold tight. Finally, we risk succumbing—sinfully, perhaps—to fear and narrowness. This surrender can fundamentally amount to a disavowal of our freedom as the children of God.

Become a Smaller, More Committed Church

When Joseph Ratzinger was once interviewed as a cardinal, he seemed to anticipate the future of the church as a smaller and more committed community of believers.[2] In one sense, his prognostication simply mirrors the sociological conclusions of Christian Smith and others. We are shrinking now, and we will be smaller in the future. In addition, the people—those who will belong to that smaller community—will belong precisely because they have stronger, more intentional, and more deliberate commitments to faith, religion, and church. The

---

[2] "Debate: Are we better off with a smaller, purer Church?," *Catholic Herald*, October 22, 2010, http://www.catholicherald.co.uk/commentandblogs/2010/10/22 /debate-are-we-better-off-with-a-smaller-purer-church/. His words cited here are: "Perhaps the time has come to say farewell to the idea of traditionally Catholic cultures. Maybe we are facing a new and different kind of epoch in the Church's history, where Christianity will again be characterised more by the mustard seed, where it will exist in small, insignificant groups that nonetheless live an intensive struggle against evil and bring the good into the world—that let God in."

faithful of this future church will know what they believe and will embrace it robustly.

The prediction of a future church that is smaller but populated by more committed believers is not absolutely guaranteed. Rather, this prediction depends on extrapolating from current trends into the future. When that extrapolation is made, it does bring us to a church of the future with fewer people and a much smaller institutional life.

It is also possible—and this is very important for our concerns— to shift *from predicting* a shrinking church in the future *to fostering* a strategy that embraces and develops a smaller but more committed church. In other words, we can speak of a shift from description to program. The response to living in a secular age and to a diminished number of participants in the life of the church would be to concentrate the energies and the people who remain into a more vibrant and deliberate community of faith. Naturally, this community would also emerge as much smaller. This strategy or program seems to be a legitimate response to the question of what we can do in a secular age with decreasing numbers of participants in the life of the church. Not only does this seem to be a legitimate response, but it also appears to be a very appealing one. At the same time, the smaller-but-better program can also be dangerous. I will explain both the appeal and danger after we consider some biblical images that have been invoked as foundational for this approach. The three biblical images that have been coupled with theological reflection are the *diaspora*, the *faithful remnant*, and the *little flock*.

The theologian Karl Rahner often spoke of the future church and believers within it as belonging to a *diaspora*,[3] like the Jews scattered and sometimes exiled outside their own land. According to Rahner, these Jews existed in ways that Catholic Christian believers will exist in the future (and, in fact, in many places already exist), that is, as scattered minority communities of faith in an otherwise religiously

---

[3] Rahner returned to the theme of diaspora in various writings. See, for example, his essay "The Christian among Unbelieving Relations," in *Theological Investigations*, vol. III, trans. Karl-H and Boniface Kruger (Baltimore: Helicon Press, 1967), 355.

alien environment. In the Bible, the legends of Daniel, for example, were meant for the Jews of the Persian diaspora. Gerhard von Rad comments, "The message they brought to their own age was an exhortation to obey the commandments of their own God precisely within the narrow limits of co-existence with the worshippers of other gods. It was also a warning: they were to be on their guard, and ready, if need be, to face very bitter hostility. For hatred of the chosen people and of their way of worship could spring up spontaneously from the very heart of these empires—their cultic philosophies."[4]

Rahner takes his cue from these biblical perspectives and then pictures the kind of Christian who can and will survive in this environment. He anticipates a lack of cultural and institutional support for Christian living. The Christian of this diaspora future will be, in his often quoted words, "a mystic or nothing at all." In other words, he underscores the essential place of interiority, of a deeply rooted spiritual life as the sine qua non of Christian existence in a nonsupportive and even hostile world.[5]

The diaspora experience—whether in biblical narratives or in Rahner's future projections—always has to do with faithful preservation of religious tradition and unstinting perseverance, generally against the odds, of a Christian way of life in the world. Religion's institutional life is never absent, but neither is it an intensely felt presence that might provide strong daily support. This description reveals Rahner's Ignatian roots and the apostolic-missionary ideals of the Society of Jesus as it pushes out to the edges of human society. We find ourselves before the Ignatian summons to be a *contemplativus in actione*, a contemplative in action, whose spirituality and very demeanor enable him or her to achieve a kind of interior freedom and independence from the vicissitudes of whatever cultural restraints might be in play.

The second image is that of the *faithful remnant*. The original sense of "remnant" belongs to the political-social world of the Bible.

[4] Gerhard von Rad, *Old Testament Theology*, vol. II: *The Theology of Israel's Prophetic Traditions*, trans. D. M. G. Stalker (London: Oliver and Boyd, 1965), 310.

[5] See Karl Rahner, "The Spirituality of the Future," in *The Practice of Faith: A Handbook of Contemporary Spirituality*, ed. K. Lehmann and A. Raffelt, trans. E. Quinn (New York: Crossroad, 1992), 21–22.

It stands, for example, for those who are left after the devastations of war and famine. In parts of the prophetic tradition, however, the notion of remnant assumes a decisive place in God's saving plan for his people. So, for example, when the prophet Elijah is on Mount Horeb (see 1 Kgs 19:11-18) lamenting that Israel has turned its back on God and that he alone has kept true faith, God reveals to him his plan. Von Rad comments, "Jahweh intends to 'leave seven thousand, all the knees that have not bowed to Baal, and every mouth that has not kissed him' (1 Kings 19:18). These words are at once the climax of the story and the key to its meaning, for they are, of course, the answer to Elijah's complaints that he was the only remaining loyal worshipper of Jahweh. There are certainly to be terrible chastisements: nevertheless an Israel will survive to stand before Jahweh. Of course—and here a new note is struck in Israel's story—it will only consist of a remnant . . . God appoints the remnant . . . (and it) doubtless consists of those who had remained faithful."[6]

The prophet Isaiah also spoke of a remnant and even named one of his sons *Shear-jashub* ("a remnant shall return," see Isa 7:3). He speaks of a repentant remnant of Israel (Isa 10:20-23) and of the remnant's restoration from exile (Isa 11:16). The faithful remnant, according to the prophets, includes those small in number whom God raises up to advance his people. They are, indeed, few. They may stand in need of repentance. By God's very own hand, however, they advance his saving plan. Echoes of the "faithful remnant" also reverberate in the New Testament. From the faithful inner circle of disciples, especially the twelve, Jesus envisions God's saving plan unfolding in time and in eternity. So, for example, he says to them at the Last Supper, "You are those who have stood by me in my trials; and I confer on you, just as my Father has conferred on me, a kingdom" (Luke 22:28-29). In another context, the Bread of Life discourse, the circle of discipleship is reduced to a small band of true believers: "Because of this many of his disciples turned back and no longer went about with him. So Jesus asked the twelve, 'Do you also wish to go away?' Simon Peter answered, 'Lord, to whom can we go?

---

[6] Von Rad, *Old Testament Theology*, vol. II, 21.

You have the words of eternal life. We have come to believe and know that you are the Holy One of God'" (John 6:66-69).

The biblical image of the faithful remnant includes some essential characteristics. The faithful remnant means, first of all, a reduced number of those who belong to the believing community. Additionally, the faith of those who do belong is highly concentrated and perhaps purified through a process of repentance. Finally, the faithful remnant has a prospect of mission or purpose beyond the community itself. In God's plan, for example, it may be destined to offer special witness to the larger world or to be a special leaven of transformation.

When the faithful remnant is viewed in this way, it can easily become a theological template for both understanding and directing ways of living out faith, religion, and church in our world today and in the future. In fact, although he has not developed this connection in explicit detail, Pope Benedict XVI's reflections on the future of the church point in the direction of the faithful remnant: smaller, more faithful, and endowed with a greater sense of mission. What remains undeveloped is a new shaping of institutional life, ways of personal and spiritual formation, and the disposition of material and personal resources.

The third biblical image is the *little flock*. The image comes from Jesus' words in Luke's gospel: "Do not be afraid, little flock, for it is your Father's good pleasure to give you the kingdom" (Luke 12:32). In John's gospel, the same image evokes a circle of intimate relationships with Jesus at the center: "I am the good shepherd. I know my own and my own know me, just as the Father knows me and I know the Father. And I lay down my life for the sheep" (John 10:14-15). This little flock experiences the danger of the wolf that would come and snatch and scatter the sheep, but the flock finds its security in its good shepherd. The sheep can and do separate themselves from the flock, but the shepherd retrieves them. "Which one of you, having a hundred sheep and losing one of them, does not leave the ninety-nine in the wilderness and go after the one that is lost until he finds it?" (Luke 15:4).

When the little flock image is translated into the life of the church, certain characteristics of the community of believers become immediately evident. The church of the little flock enjoys a particular intimacy or closeness with Jesus and with other believers. It is a small circle of believers sustained by reciprocal knowledge, knowing Jesus and being known by him. It is also a community of repentance and return, a place of homecoming after one has strayed. It is a community that travels cautiously in a world that is beset with dangerous and destructive forces.

The church of the little flock permeates the New Testament. It is, for example, evident in the circle of disciples during the public ministry of Jesus. It is also the small and concentrated communities of faith that Paul addresses in his letters. They have minority status in a larger and generally alien world. The challenge of navigating a hostile and even destructive world appears clearly in the Pastoral Epistles and the book of Revelation.

The biblical image of the little flock does not yield a specific program for the future of faith, religion, and church. It does, however, highlight particular features and emphases of that future and smaller church. For example, a *distinctive identity* as the little flock marks and shapes the church. There is no mistaking this community for any other gathering of people. An *abiding Christocentrism* also marks and shapes the church. Jesus is the community's unique resource in sustaining and growing in its life together. Finally, the little flock church must necessarily engage the world in which it lives, but its engagement is cautious, limited, and always under the protective mantle of the shepherd.

A smaller, more committed church: The right direction? After examining the prospects for faith, religion, and church from the perspectives of philosophy, history, cultural studies, and sociology, we raised the question, what can we do? The first response to that question was to do nothing new but rather to stay on course, in other words, to continue doing what we have always been doing. Reflection on that course of nonaction identified why it might be a reasonable option but an inadequate one. The second response that we have just now considered in this section took a different turn. This response indicated that we can foster or promote a smaller and a more committed church that would rely on the intentional and deliberate faith of those who belong to it. The research data suggest that faith, religion, and church are shrinking. The second response accepts that fact and then, in effect, engineers the shrinking so that it doesn't just happen but so that it follows patterns of deeper and more intentional commitment. The biblical images coupled with theological reflection—*diaspora*, *remnant*, and *little flock*—offer a foundation but not a complete rationale for this direction. In fact, the smaller-but-better strategy needs critical review. Earlier, I said that this approach is appealing but also potentially dangerous. Now, we need to identify the benefits and the potential for negative outcomes.

First, it may be helpful to put the movement toward a smaller and more committed church in a historical context. This direction represents a reversal of a pastoral decision that began with the conversion of the Germanic tribes about sixteen hundred years ago. At that time, there was a shift from a deliberate and intentional Christian commitment—an obvious consequence of the age of persecutions—to what has been called "massive Christianity" that incorporated many new converts with a hope that catechesis would follow later.[7] The pattern of massive Christianity has continued into our own day, although the introduction of the *Rite of Christian Initiation of Adults* after the Second Vatican Council signaled a shift of direction to a more deliberate and intentional Christian commitment.

Now we can return to the benefits and potential negative outcomes for what I have called the smaller-but-better strategy for faith, religion, and especially church. We begin with the benefits and appeal of this strategy. The movement to more deliberate and intentional faith commitments has a bracing clarity about it. If you recall the difficulty that Christian Smith had in identifying who actually qualified to be called "Catholic," then you realize that the boundaries now become firmer and clearer when everyone who carries the name Catholic does so quite deliberately. From the perspective of institutional management, or what theological language would call church governance, there is a greater ease of operation, because leadership (and those who follow) clearly know what to expect. Finally, given the countercultural quality of this deliberate and intentional commitment, faith, religion,

[7] See, for example, Albert Mirgeler, *Mutations of Western Christianity*, trans. E. Quinn (London: Burns and Oates, 1964), especially 44–65.

and church may even embrace a heroic dimension that comes with standing apart from the crowd. All this amounts to something beneficial and certainly appealing.

Smaller and more intentional and deliberate, however, may not always be better. This approach can harbor and foster negative tendencies with which Christianity has struggled across two thousand years. The deliberate and intentional threshold for commitment can make faith, religion, and church exclusionary and elitist. Historically, this has led to struggles with Gnosticism (an elite circle of initiates), Novatianism and Donatism (rigidly unforgiving of human failure), Jansenism (a rigoristic moralism), and—more generally—perfectionism that makes little or no allowance for a genuine journey of spiritual growth.

If this smaller, more deliberate, and more intentional church that aspires to be a purer church then capitulates to perfectionistic tendencies, it will be a countersign to that community that Jesus envisioned as the seed of the coming of the reign of God. There are two important parables unique to Matthew's gospel, which is known as the "ecclesiastical gospel," the parable of the weeds among the wheat (Matt 13:24-30 and see 13:36-43) and the parable of the dragnet cast into the sea (Matt 13:47-50). Both parables teach that in the present age the community of Jesus' followers is not a uniformly perfect community. It includes weeds among the wheat and bad fish among the good. Resolution of these inconsistencies comes not in this world at this time but in the future and by God's hand. In the meanwhile, any authentic future direction for the church must take into account what is not usually included in the study of the church known as ecclesiology. And that is a state of messiness, while we are on our pilgrim way in the world.

At this point, we may feel caught on the horns of a dilemma. The biblical images of *diaspora, remnant,* and *little flock* seem to encourage us in the direction of a smaller, more deliberate, and more intentional faith commitment and church life. At the same time, the elitist and exclusionary mentality that this smaller and more intense commitment can generate contradicts the inclusive and sometimes messy reality of the community of Jesus' followers. How do we reconcile these two seemingly opposed directions?

In a final proposal—which is a third response to the question of what we can do—I will in the next chapter try to incorporate the positive directions offered by the biblical images, while, at the same time, respecting the church as an inclusive, receptive, and hospitable community of faith. In the meanwhile, however, it may be helpful to recognize that the same church can contain both the smaller-more-committed community and, at the same time, the larger and perhaps somewhat disheveled community of believers. How is this possible?

If we consider the place and the contribution of religious life in the church, we can begin to understand how a more deliberate and more intentional commitment and community serves the larger church *from within*. The following passage from the Second Vatican Council's Dogmatic Constitution on the Church, *Lumen Gentium*, describes this reality:

> The religious state of life, in bestowing greater freedom from the cares of earthly existence on those who follow it, simultaneously reveals more clearly to all believers the heavenly goods which are already present in this age, witnessing to the new and eternal life which we have acquired through the redemptive work of Christ and preluding our future resurrection and the glory of the heavenly kingdom. Furthermore the religious state constitutes a closer imitation and an abiding reenactment in the Church of the form of life which the Son of God made his own when he came into the world to do the will of the Father and which he propounded to the disciples who followed him. Finally this state manifests in a special way the transcendence of the kingdom of God and its requirements over all earthly things . . . , bringing home to all men [and women] the immeasurable greatness of the power of Christ in his sovereignty and the infinite might of the Holy Spirit which works so marvelously in the Church. (LG 44)

And just as religious life takes up and lives out the biblical images of *diaspora, faithful remnant,* and *little flock,* so too lay ecclesial movements with their emphasis on intentionality and community bring their grace to the interior life of the church. Now, we can consider a third proposal of what we, the larger community of faith, can do, as we move into the future.

4

What *Ought* We to Do?

Reclaim the Dynamism of the Gospel:
Be Evangelized and Evangelizing

We have been considering faith, religion, and church. When we view these realities through the lens of philosophy, history, and the human sciences, the future prospects for faith, religion, and church look dim. All the indicators point to decline. We have begun to explore how people of faith in the church might respond and move into the future. The first two responses included doing nothing new, which means continuing on the current course and, secondly, programming or fostering a smaller but more committed church with fewer members but deeper faith. The first response is understandable but clearly inadequate. The second response enjoys some biblical foundations and has elements of merit, but it also carries a potential for major problems. At this point, I want to introduce a third response that incorporates some elements of the second but greatly expands our outreach as church. This third response incorporates the fundamental dynamism of evangelization.

In the interest of full disclosure, let me be honest about my sense of evangelization. Whenever I hear the word "evangelization," I hesitate. Why is that? Evangelization certainly has a venerable history in the church, and in recent decades it is proposed as the great task and responsibility of the church in many official documents and in theological writing. My hesitation, however, to identify it as the response to the complex circumstances of our life and culture today stems from common but shallow understandings of evangelization that seem often to prevail. For example, frequently evangelization seems identified with a friendly and enthusiastic but fundamentally superficial presentation of Jesus to the world. For many people in church ministry, evangelization is often linked to the latest program for parish or church renewal that claims to be the *ne plus ultra* tool for recruiting more people and boosting the number of congregants.

In fact, evangelization and its dynamism, correctly and completely understood, can provide the energy and direction to respond to our complex cultural, social, and religious circumstances today and into the future. But it must be correctly and completely understood. The key insight for an adequate sense of evangelization comes to us from Blessed Paul VI's 1975 apostolic exhortation, *Evangelii Nuntiandi* (On Evangelization in the Modern World). He identifies the church as an *evangelized* and, at the same time, *evangelizing* community. Thirty-eight years later in *Evangelii Gaudium*, Pope Francis reaffirms this insight, when he speaks of the church as a community of *missionary* (evangelizing) *disciples* (evangelized).[1]

It is very important to note that being evangelized and evangelizing are not sequential and linear events, as if once we were evangelized we can then go forward to evangelize. Rather, being evangelized and evangelizing are both *continuous,* in the sense that they are permanent states of the church, and *simultaneous,* in the sense that they are distinguishable but never separated from each other. We will consider this sense of the church as evangelized and evangelizing in greater detail shortly. First, we can note four moments of evangelization that apply to the church both as evangelized and evangelizing.

It is abundantly clear, although not spelled out explicitly, in *Evangelii Nuntiandi* and *Evangelii Gaudium* that there are four essential moments in evangelization, four moments that correspond to two questions and two invitations found in the gospel. They are (1) *What are you looking for?*—the fundamental question of human searching; (2) *Come and see*—the invitation to see Jesus and to be introduced to him; (3) *Are you going to stay?*—the question of decision and

---

[1] Pope Francis, *Evangelii Gaudium* 120, 122, 164.

sustained commitment; and (4) *Go and proclaim the Good News*—
the invitation and call addressed to the entire community of believers
to go forward and to carry on their evangelizing mission and purpose.
The church, simultaneously evangelized and evangelizing, hears and
responds to these questions and invitations and then carries them
into the world. In this way, the dynamism of the Gospel continues to
provide the spiritual motivation and the holy direction to go forward
and to engage the world. Again, we will return to these essential
moments to consider them in greater detail. For now, this provides
an overview. Before that more detailed consideration, notice how
this dynamism of evangelization incorporates the strategy of greater
commitment that belongs to the second response, while still holding
open the sense of inclusion and generosity by inviting all people.

See what happens when the church keeps asking itself and the
world the question, *What are you looking for?* When the church keeps
saying to itself and the world, *Come and see.* When the church keeps
asking itself and the world, *Are you going to stay?* When the church
keeps telling itself and the world, *Go and proclaim the Good News.*
As these four moments occur, some, perhaps few, will "get it." This
can be the small-but-committed community of faith that we identified earlier. Some, perhaps many, will not get it. They may even
come into the community of faith or be born into it but not practice
very much or at all. They don't get it, or they refuse to get it. They
will, however, in this understanding of evangelization hear it again
and again and again, because the church and its members will not
tire at each juncture and in every encounter to keep repeating these
questions and invitations. The opportunities to come to true faith
in the community of the church do not cease. In this pattern, real
faith and an exclusive and full commitment are concentrated. At
the same time, nothing is lost of the inclusive invitation extended
to everyone, in other words, to that "whole world" and to "all the
nations" to which the risen Lord sends his disciples.

Finally, before we examine the identity of the church as evangelized and evangelizing and the four moments of that evangelization, I want to suggest how this approach eliminates religion as
an obstacle to faith. The German Lutheran theologian and pastor
Dietrich Bonhoeffer spoke of "religionless Christianity." Religion for

Bonhoeffer—and this aligns well with his Lutheran heritage—could easily become for people today who live in "a world come of age" an impediment to encountering Christ and embracing true faith. For him, the institutions, the rituals, and the precepts of organized religion often amounted to a blockage of our access to Christ and the true essence of Christianity. He saw this as a particular problem that beset Catholics: "We cannot, like the Roman Catholics, simply identify ourselves with the church."[2] Granted that Bonhoeffer did not have a refined or nuanced understanding of a Catholic sense of sacramentality and the integral relationship of the church as spiritual communion and organized institution, his warning that religious structures can obscure rather than illuminate a genuine relationship with Jesus Christ is a point well taken. And it is one that many of our contemporaries take to heart. In fact, as we noted earlier, people may be ready to be believers but not necessarily belongers. They say, for example, that they are spiritual but not religious. Still, another model is possible, as we look at the relationship of church, religion, and evangelization. The central dynamism of the church as evangelized and, simultaneously, evangelizing—always freshly encountering the Christ who will be proclaimed to others—enables us to move beyond the need for a "religionless Christianity." The church and religion get "unstuck" from a merely organizational, institutional, and structural mold. Again, we will consider this in greater detail shortly.

The Church Evangelized and Evangelizing

We can now return to reflect more deeply on the centrality of the church as both continuously evangelized and always evangelizing. First, we must note the overall relationship of the church to evangelization. The synod of 1974, Blessed Paul VI in *Evangelii Nuntiandi*, St. John Paul II especially in *Redemptoris Missio* (On the Permanent Validity of the Church's Missionary Mandate), Pope Benedict XVI especially in *Verbum Domini* (The Word of the Lord), and Pope Francis in *Evangelii Gaudium* locate the central identity and purpose of

---

[2] See Dietrich Bonhoeffer, *Letters and Papers from Prison*, enlarged ed., trans. R. Fuller et al. (New York: Macmillan, 1972), 279–80, 380–83, especially 382.

the church in evangelization. Paul VI writes, "at the end of the great Assembly of 1974 we heard these illuminating words: 'We wish to confirm once more that the task of evangelizing all people constitutes the essential mission of the Church.' It is a task and mission which the vast and profound changes of present-day society make all the more urgent. Evangelizing is in fact the grace and vocation proper to the Church, her deepest identity. She exists in order to evangelize" (*Evangelii Nuntiandi* 14).

These statements linking the church's central identity and essential purpose with evangelization come to us with a welcome clarity, but they are not fundamentally surprising. The next set of affirmations, however, is astonishing. Now, the popes in their apostolic exhortations on evangelization say that not only is the church the agent of evangelization but that the church itself stands in constant need of being evangelized. Bringing the Gospel to the world means continuously receiving that Gospel anew in the life of the church. Paul VI says, "The Church is an evangelizer, but she begins by being evangelized herself. She is the community of believers . . . and she needs to listen unceasingly to what she must believe . . . In brief, this means that she has a constant need of being evangelized, if she wishes to retain freshness, vigor and strength in order to proclaim the Gospel . . . the Church . . . is evangelized by constant conversion and renewal in order to evangelize the world with credibility" (*Evangelii Nuntiandi* 15). Pope Francis expresses this thought even more directly: "The Church does not evangelize unless she constantly lets herself be evangelized" (*Evangelii Gaudium* 174).

To accept, to understand, and then to live the reality of church as a community that is simultaneously and continuously evangelized and evangelizing sets us in a very new horizon or, at least, one that is newly identified. It taps a dynamism that has always been a part of the life of the church but not always recognized, appreciated, and lived. Think, for example, of the great saints of our tradition. Francis of Assisi evangelized, because he was continuously being evangelized—continuously encountering and coming to know anew the living Christ.

The evangelized-evangelizing dynamic answers the question of how we shall be the church in the world, and it does so in a surprising way. Most people, whether inside or outside the church, view the church as a community or institution that brings something to the world—a message, a way of life, a set of rituals. The evangelized-evangelizing dynamic reframes that perspective. As church we not only go out to the world to give it something, but together with the world we receive something—the word of life. This means that the action of evangelization embeds the community of faith in the very world that is to be evangelized. The church, then, does not stand in a line with other ideologies that promise a key to life, happiness, authenticity, or whatever the human heart seeks. We are uniquely joined in solidarity with that world, just as Jesus was in solidarity with the ones whom he served, just as he shared with his listeners the radical call to fulfill the Father's will. In this experience of evangelization, the church needs to assume a humble stance, the very opposite of that of an aggressive agent of proselytizing or a condescending donor of heavenly goods.

This astonishing and dynamic relationship of church and world centered in evangelization began to be articulated by Paul VI in his encyclical *Ecclesiam Suam*,[3] which he wrote as the second session of the Second Vatican Council began. His call for dialogue and reciprocity with the world only makes sense if we understand church and world not as two opposing forces but, ultimately, as two realities bound together by the life-giving word of God.

Everything noted in the first part of our reflections, for example, about living in a secular age, takes on new shape in light of the evangelized-evangelizing dynamic. We are inheritors of oppositional and adversarial stances that church and world have assumed as they faced each other. In fact, church and world do stand in contrast to each other in many significant ways. As a believer, I can say that it clearly matters if God is denied, if human freedom is reduced to a license to do whatever, and if human life is treated without the great dignity and reverence that it deserves—positions that commonly belong to those who live in a secular age or are often ascribed to them. To be true to my faith, I cannot accept these conclusions, and

---

[3] Paul VI, *Ecclesiam Suam* (On the Church), August 6, 1964.

I hope that the truth I have come to know and accept about God, freedom, and life could be shared with others. At the same time and at a deeper and more fundamental level of existence, I, too, am being evangelized. The questions of God, of freedom, and of life are alive for me. And these questions are alive for those outside of the family of faith, albeit in different form. In being continuously evangelized, I do grapple with those same questions and challenges that have given birth to a secular age. We are together, not necessarily in our conclusions but in a common quest and search. For me, the light of the Gospel makes all the difference in the quest and search, as I am evangelized. And I can, from the common quest and search, begin to share the light, as I evangelize. The breakthrough of connection—and it is at a very deep level—moves us beyond what have become predictable and futile adversarial and oppositional stances.

A final observation drawn from the gospels may help to understand the essential importance of the evangelized-evangelizing dynamic. From one perspective, the gospels are a narrative of the formation of Jesus' earliest disciples. That narrative has perennial paradigmatic value. Each generation comes to know how to become disciples of Jesus by watching the process in the gospels. A very striking description of discipleship emerges in chapter 3 of Mark's gospel, when Jesus appoints the Twelve: "And he appointed twelve, whom he also named apostles, to be with him, and to be sent out to proclaim the message, and to have authority to cast out demons" (Mark 3:14-15). There is a twofold and, initially, paradoxical dimension attached to the call of the Twelve. They are to be with him and to be sent out from him. How can they both be with him and, at the same time, be sent out from him? Ought it to not be one or the other, either they are present with him and to him, or they are sent out from him? The text insists that both are true. The ones whom Jesus chooses are simultaneously to be with him as his disciples who keep learning from him by receiving his word. At the same time, they are his apostles who are sent from him and serve as missionaries carrying the word to others. In other words, we see here and throughout the gospels the very same dynamic of being evangelized and evangelizing at work in the community of those who follow Jesus. These verses from Mark evidently demonstrate the disciple-apostle or evangelized-evangelizing dynamic, but, clearly, the pattern remains evident throughout all the gospels. Finally, this description of the earliest community around Jesus is normative and formative for every subsequent generation of those who want to belong to the Lord and follow him.

The Questions and Invitations

The act, event, or process of evangelization—both as being evangelized and evangelizing—has a distinctive shape. As the gospels present it and as church teaching explains it, evangelization has four moments that we can identify as two questions and two invitations: (1) *What are you looking for?* (2) *Come and see.* (3) *Are you going to stay?* (4) *Go and proclaim the Good News.*

We have already cited Paul VI, who said, "Evangelizing is in fact the grace and vocation proper to the Church, her deepest identity." This means that the very mission and authenticity of the church hinge on whether or not it assumes its proper identity and mission by evangelizing and, of course, also by simultaneously being evangelized. This, in turn, means that the two gospel-based questions and the two gospel-based invitations are continuously circulating within the church *ad intra* or on the inside. It also means the church is continuously bringing these questions and invitations to the world *ad extra* or outside of itself.

Earlier we reflected on the state of the world and the state of the church. Then we extrapolated this reality into the future. The church, it seems, will live in a secular age with declining numbers, at least in North America and Europe. We understood that there are multiple options available to the church, the community of faith, although two of the available options are completely or partially negative. For example, staying on the current course, whether from inertia or a failure of nerve, was unacceptable. Fostering a smaller but more committed church had positive features but carried a risk of elitism, something that is entirely foreign to the Gospel message. The third path of evangelization, properly and completely understood, seems to be the authentic direction for the future, and the one that we ought to take. At the same time, that evangelization—again understood as being evangelized and evangelizing—will take place in the secular age that we earlier described. The task now before us is to describe how the questions and invitations that constitute the process of evangelization will look in that secular context. And it is, of course, not simply a matter of description. We also need to identify how we will engage the process, what action we will take.

What Are You Looking For? (See John 1:38)

Questions in general and the particular question *What are you looking for?* belong to that phase of evangelization that Paul VI calls "pre-evangelization." The questions open people to hearing the word of life. The questions themselves arrive into the lives of people in different ways, and they broach a wide variety of concerns. Of course, evangelizers themselves, if they are truly to be continuously evangelized, face the very same questions, so that the word they bring to others may take even deeper root in their own lives.

A first set of questions stems from the witness of believers. Here is how Paul VI describes this process:

> Let us suppose that . . . they [Christian believers] radiate in an altogether simple and unaffected way their faith in values that go beyond current values, and their hope in something that is not seen and that would not dare to imagine. Through this wordless witness these Christians stir up irresistible questions in the hearts of those who see how they live: why are they like this? Why do they live this way? Who or what is it that inspires them? Why are they in our midst? . . . Other questions will arise, deeper and more demanding ones, questions evoked by this witness which involves presence, sharing, solidarity, and which is an essential element, and generally the first one, in evangelization. (*Evangelii Nuntiandi* 21)

Evangelizers can also raise a second set of questions. In this instance, evangelizers make explicit those great and universal existential questions that belong to all people, especially as they face their finitude and mortality: what will contribute to my well-being? What will offer me fulfillment? How can I find happiness? Evangelizers can also take a cue from St. Paul as he reflects on his own experience of inner division in a way that also mirrors common human experience:

"I do not understand my own actions. For I do not do what I want, but I do the very thing I hate. . . For I do not do the good I want, but the evil I do not want is what I do. Now if I do what I do not want, it is no longer I that do it, but sin that dwells within me. . . . Who will rescue me from this body of death?" (Rom 7:15, 19-20, 24).

Paul VI also identifies a third set of questions that evangelizers pose to their listeners. The way of posing the questions is oblique. The intent is to create a space for what will later come as an explicit proclamation of the Gospel. The questions and groundwork are laid out in "art, the scientific approach, philosophical research and legitimate recourse to the sentiments of the human heart" (*Evangelii Nuntiandi* 51).

A more direct line of questions emerges from the concerns and the discontents that simmer just below the surface for our contemporaries in the secular age. The themes of this fourth set of questions have to do with *sexuality*, the *social order, politics, economics,* modern *communications,* and the *environment.* In so many ways, these are the hot-button issues of the secular age. Why? They capture the great themes of secularity that include individuality, self-expression, freedom to shape one's life, and strategies for survival with the consequences of science and technology. There is a secular mindset that claims to address the themes of these questions. And, in fact, that is true. The difficulty, however, rests in the insufficiency and incompleteness of the secular response to these questions that press on fundamental human concerns and longings. Effective evangelization critically reviews the themes and sharpens the questions to indicate the gap between our human aspirations and the contemporary responses to them that a closed-ended and, frankly, often smug secularity claims to be complete. In other words, evangelization takes up the themes, sharpens the questions, and raises the underlying question, *What are you really looking for?* We can consider each of these themes and, at least, briefly raise the kind of questions that a process of evangelization would raise to create an "open space" for the proclamation of the word of life.

The theme of *sexuality* occupies an important place in a secular age, especially in a post-pill, a post-Roe v. Wade, and an ascendant gay rights world. And the secular directions set for human sexuality have had significant impact in reshaping marriage and family life.[4] Historically, the church as a faith community has generally been inclined to offer a moral analysis of the inadequacy of contemporary takes on human sexuality as a first response. If, however, the church begins by engaging the theme of contemporary human sexuality from its responsibility for evangelization, the church's intervention will look much different. It will be in the order of questions that are the result of a careful and critical reflection that reveals the inadequacy of contemporary understandings and practices of human sexuality. It will pick up that great question of evangelization, *What are you looking for?* It will, for example, address those immersed in the secular culture's ethos of sexuality with this question: With your sexual freedom, are you now happier, healthier, more intimate, and more fulfilled than before you had this freedom? In fact, there are gaps and discontents for everyone, including those who consider themselves most liberated. The point of this question is to sharpen the human search that can open a path to receiving the word of life. Obviously, what is given here by way of theme and question is a compressed version of something that needs much further elaboration.

The secular age, as Charles Taylor has described it, envisions an evolved *social order* that is suffused by Jean-Jacques Rousseau's sense of the natural goodness of nature, including human nature. Contemporary experience, however, speaks of human environments that are anything but good. Many people find themselves in situations of forced separation and isolation from others, especially those of other classes. Many encounter violence of the most severe kind as a reality of daily life. Questions need to be raised. Why do human beings turn on each other? Is it simply in our nature to be in conflict with each other? Is it possible to have a different kind of future for humanity, one that includes connection, solidarity, and peace? These questions reveal a social dimension of human searching and longing. They also belie the immanent sufficiency of humanity to organize

---

[4] See *Evangelii Gaudium* 65–67; and especially Pope Francis, *Amoris Laetitia* (The Joy of Love), March 19, 2016, chap. 2, "The Experiences and Challenges of Families," 31–57.

itself rationally for a uniformly peaceable existence. Again, a path opens for the word of life.

Similarly, the contemporary *political order*, in a phenomenon that crosses over national boundaries, suffers from an inability to foster collaboration for the common good. With multiple grabs for power, the political process stymies citizens, and all the people suffer. Governments cannot seem to work to create those just and equitable environments in which people can flourish. This easily fosters corruption and a general sense of alienation that can erupt in violence. Even apart from its most disastrous consequences, the failure of politics and civil governance breeds a pervasive spirit of cynicism and deeply and dangerously discontented populations. The question of politics is simple and vitally important. How can we arrive at a point of shedding our individual self-interest in a process of learning how to collaborate together for the common good? This question chips away at a worldview that fails to take into account a higher purpose in our lives that transcends the socially suffocating boundaries of self-interest. The question also reveals, as Jürgen Habermas indicated earlier, the secular gap in preserving "an essential connection to the ongoing practice of life within a community."[5] In that way, questions raised because of the failures of the political order engage the human quest for the good life together by laying open prospects for another way of being together. And the question anticipates a response to be given with the proclamation of the word of life.

Economic life in a secular environment generally runs on the steam of often mindless (think "irrational exuberance") and generally valueless processes that yield unpredictable bounty for some (usually, few) and straitened circumstances for many. In other words, the goods needed to live and to live well get irrationally apportioned. The inequity of this situation generates social unrest. Ironically, the humanistic values of a secular age are belied in the way that contemporary and thoroughly secular economies work. In the words of Pope Francis, we face "the idolatry of money and the dictatorship of an impersonal economy lacking a truly human purpose" (*Evangelii*

---

[5] Jürgen Habermas et al., *An Awareness of What is Missing: Faith and Reason in a Post-Secular Age*, trans. C. Cronin (Malden, MA: Polity Press, 2010), 75.

Gaudium 55). Evangelization raises a fundamental critical question that has universal scope: Why can we not make it possible that everyone has enough of everything necessary to live well in a world that we know is richly endowed with more than sufficient material goods? This straightforward human question creates a space for probing fundamental questions of value and willingness to engage in a sense of higher purpose. That space for reflection, in turn, belongs not only to economic reasoning but to new possibilities uncovered by the word of life.

Similar to economic life, *mass media and electronic communications* roll on their own energy that is fueled by whatever is technologically possible and whatever appeals to the market. They can promote social goods that include connecting people with each other, informing people about their world, and entertaining large audiences. They can construct immense networks of connection. Additionally, mass media and electronic communications capture a central value and dynamic of secular culture—the possibility of expression and, especially, self-expression. Along with their powerful constructive possibilities, not surprisingly, mass media and electronic communications can take a negative turn. If manipulated to misinform, they have a destructive potential. If used as the only means of communication and connection, they can paradoxically leave people isolated and alone behind a screen. In this context, evangelization can and ought to utilize what mass media and electronic communications have to offer to bring the word of life to people. The evangelization process must also raise critical questions that expose negative potentials and insufficiency. A fundamental question might be, In an electronic age, what does it take to foster a true human encounter that connects people in truth? The question assumes appearances of connection and encounter that may not match the reality. Real encounter and communication can only happen in the truth of who we are, and that includes a transcendent dimension. Again, the question opens a space for proclaiming the word of life as a foundation for human communication and connection.

A final theme for questions is the *environment*. It seems that we live in an increasingly degraded environment that, long-term without a significant modification of our current practices, will not be able to sustain life, especially human life. The humanistic values of a secular age have urged us to develop the world and its resources for our benefit. Paradoxically, so many of our efforts of development have resulted in the degradation that threatens our environment. We often feel caught between short-term benefits and long-term consequences. The larger sense of purpose and motivation for protecting and healing the environment appears to be missing. It also seems difficult to bring together ecological concerns for the planet with ecology that incorporates and integrates the human person. Many of the challenges are new and unfamiliar, and the values at stake in these challenges are not precisely identified. All this suggests the need for critical reflection and the development of questions that can be brought to bear on our situation in the world. A process of evangelization can initiate the questions, such as, "Ultimately, what responsibility sustains us in our commitment to develop and preserve the natural resources given to us in the world? What are the deep and lasting resources for such a commitment?" The question already hints that these resources transcend our role as "consumers" in this world and direct us to our responsibility that is entrusted to us as "stewards."[6] Again, space is created to proclaim the word of life.

When we review all these questions, clarity emerges. In the course of human life and searching, we grapple with sexuality, the social order, the political order, economic life, communications, and the environment. In its own way, the secular age provides frameworks and directions for all these contexts. In some measure, those secular approaches may be helpful, but as we explore each theme, we also discover that in a purely and closed-ended secular context they are incomplete. There is more to be had. A process of evangelization raises that "more to be had" as a way of creating or opening space where the word of life may be proclaimed. And all this fits into the larger context of human questions that we also considered, such as the questions raised by Christian witness in the world and the perennial and existential questions about happiness, hope, and integrity of our lives.

---

[6] See *Evangelii Gaudium* 215; for a complete treatment of these questions see Pope Francis, *Laudato Si* (On Care for Our Common Home), May 24, 2015.

The evangelized and evangelizing community of faith raises these questions for itself as the church and for the world that is the field in which the seed of the word will be planted. These multiple questions correspond to that one momentous question that Jesus poses to the two disciples of John the Baptist: *What are you looking for?*

The questions that we have identified transpose Jesus' question into the circumstances of our life today. They aim to bring people to a point of openness to receiving what follows, the invitation to come and see Jesus. What remains is to determine *how* they are to be asked. If evangelizers pose the questions in a didactic or discursive way, that is, abstractly, the questions will probably never reach their intended audience. The questions need to be offered in an imaginative and personally engaging format. I have no formulas for that, but I would suggest that we draw both on our history in the church and on today's patterns of "rich cultural production" (the words of James Davison Hunter) to find models. Across the centuries, the church has communicated in a variety of imaginative ways. Take, for example, the medieval mystery plays. The dramas both focused human questions and dilemmas and, then, offered the perspective of faith. If we look at today's rich cultural production, we can find examples of what can be done. Terrence Malick's film *The Tree of Life* is an instructive example that combines extraordinary cinematography with raw experiences of human longing and questions that point to transcendence.

Come and See (See John 1:39)

If the question *What are you looking for?* effectively engages people of this secular age and opens a space for them to hear the word of life, then the invitation *Come and see* can follow. Consider what this invitation means.

Come and see, in the context of John's gospel, is a very particular kind of invitation. It is an invitation to meet Jesus or to be introduced to him and then to see him or contemplate him and, eventually, come to believe in him. In other words, the invitation is about a personal encounter that leads to an extended experience of the person of Jesus, seeing him or watching him, believing in him, and, implicitly, learning from him as his disciple.

Evangelization has always meant proclaiming Jesus Christ. This involves the fundamental announcement of the Good News. The content of the message as Pope Francis encapsulates it is "the personal love of God who became man, who gave himself up for us, who is living and who offers us his salvation and his friendship" (*Evangelii Gaudium* 128). Proclamation is decisive for evangelization. The question is, how does the invitation *Come and see* connect with proclamation?

Paul VI says, for example, that our daily and generally silent witness to the Christian life in itself is insufficient, because it is implicit. Witness needs to be "made explicit by a clear and unequivocal proclamation of the Lord Jesus. The Good News proclaimed by the witness of life sooner or later has to be proclaimed by the word of life. There is no true evangelization if the name, the teaching, the life, the promises, the Kingdom and the mystery of Jesus Christ, the Son of God are not proclaimed. . . . This proclamation—*kerygma*, preaching or catechesis—occupies such an important place in evangelization that it has often become synonymous with it; and yet it is only one aspect of evangelization" (*Evangelii Nuntiandi* 22). Clearly, the proclamation entails the communication of a message, and yet the delivery of a message is itself not the sum and substance of the proclamation. The whole goal and purpose of proclamation is the presentation not of *a message about Jesus* but rather *an introduction to Jesus himself*. This introduction means bringing those who have been invited to encounter Jesus, to receive him, to believe in him, and to contemplate him. Personal introduction is an essential aspect of evangelization. It has—in my estimation—often been poorly understood or not understood at all. It deserves our closest attention. And perhaps the best way to pay attention to it is to observe and hear the greatest missionary-evangelizer of the church's history, St. Paul.

When Paul proclaims Christ Jesus, he does not simply deliver a message about Jesus, although he certainly does do that. More significantly and more fundamentally, Paul presents the living Christ to his audiences. He introduces them to the one who is crucified and risen, the one whom they can meet, and the one in whom they can live. Paul communicates Christ to his listeners and then, quite naturally, he speaks about him. This pattern is especially evident in two of his letters that reveal many autobiographical details of his apostolic life, his first and second letters to the Corinthians.

At the beginning of the second chapter of his First Letter to the Corinthians, Paul shares a very important reminiscence of his initial ministry among the Corinthians: "When I came among you, brothers and sisters, I did not come proclaiming the mystery of God to you in lofty words or wisdom. For I decided to know nothing among you except Jesus Christ, and him crucified. And I came to you in weakness and in fear and in much trembling. My speech and my proclamation were not with plausible words or wisdom, but with a demonstration of the Spirit and of power, so that your faith might rest not on human wisdom but on the power of God" (1 Cor 2:1-5). Paul's proclamation of the mystery of God to the Corinthians is not, in the first place, the delivery of a message "in lofty words or wisdom." It is, first of all, the living and risen presence of the crucified one. That presence is enabled by the Spirit and the power of God. In brief, Paul brings the person of Christ to the community. That is his evangelization, his proclamation of the Good News.

Later in the same letter, Paul describes how the living Christ who is sacramentally present can be encountered, believed, and accepted. Again, this is not a message about Jesus Christ but the proclamation and evocation of his very presence among us:

> The cup of blessing that we bless, is it not a sharing in the blood of Christ? The bread that we break, is it not a sharing in the body of Christ? . . . [T]he Lord Jesus on the night when he was betrayed took a loaf of bread, and when he had given thanks, he broke it and said, "This is my body that is for you. Do this in remembrance of me." In the same way he took the cup also, after supper, saying, "This cup is the new covenant in my blood. Do this, as often as you drink it, in remembrance of me." For as often as you eat this bread and drink this cup, you proclaim the Lord's death until he comes. (1 Cor 10:16; 11:23-26)

It is not surprising that Paul would evangelize and make proclamation primarily through a presentation or introduction of Jesus who is to be encountered, believed, and accepted directly, rather than through the delivery of a message about him. That pattern corresponds exactly to the narrative of his conversion. He did not receive a message or announcement that he then believed. As he describes his conversion experience, he found himself face-to-face with the living Christ. "Last of all, as to someone untimely born, he appeared also to me" (1 Cor 15:8). That encounter begins his journey of faith.

We have been considering the second moment of evangelization, the invitation *Come and see.* This invitation decisively shapes the explicit proclamation of Jesus Christ, which Paul VI has identified as essential for evangelization. Almost instinctively, when we hear "proclamation," we think first of the communication of a message. In fact, although there is a necessary place for messages, the primary object of proclamation in the process of evangelization is the presentation of the living Christ to people, so that they can come and see him and, by God's grace and their free decision, come to know and believe in him. The challenge, which we will consider shortly, is to identify exactly how it happens that we can proclaim and communicate a person who has died and been raised and who does not seem to have any physical markers in this world. Before we take up that challenge, I invite you to briefly consider three other biblical passages that illuminate this process of evangelization.

The end of Matthew's gospel is called "the Great Commission." Jesus' apostles gathered on a mountain to receive this commission, just before he is taken from their sight. These last words of the gospel express the basic mandate given to the entire church to evangelize: "And Jesus came and said to them, 'All authority in heaven and on earth has been given to me. Go therefore and make disciples of all nations, baptizing them in the name of the Father and of the Son and of the Holy Spirit, and teaching them to obey everything that I have commanded you. And remember, I am with you always, to the end of the age'" (Matt 28:18-20). Notice that the purpose of the apostles' mission as they go is to "make disciples." This includes the delivery of a message but also moves well beyond that. In making disciples, the apostles are bringing people of all the nations into a living relationship with Jesus, who promises, "I am with you always."

In a more oblique way, we can see the same pattern of evangelization in Peter's words to the crowd on Pentecost (Acts 2:14-36). Peter announces a message: "that God has made him both Lord and

Messiah, this Jesus whom you crucified" (Acts 2:36). Peter, however, does not simply talk about the reality of Jesus' lordship. He invites his listeners to see and hear the experience of the Lord's presence in the power of the Holy Spirit that he has poured out in his followers. Peter says, "This Jesus God raised up, and of that all of us are witnesses. Being therefore exalted at the right hand of God, and having received from the Father the promise of the Holy Spirit, he has poured out this that you both see and hear" (Acts 2:32-33). In these verses, we hear a real possibility of connection with the living Christ. And implied in these words is the invitation to come and see and believe.

A final passage comes to us from the beginning of the First Letter of John. The author draws on a direct experience of the word of life in all its tangible and visible dimensions to share that experience with others. The purpose of that sharing is to bring the listeners into a direct relationship with the Father and Jesus Christ. Again, a message is shared. Then, those who accept the testimony are drawn into a living relationship with the Lord:

> We declare to you what was from the beginning, what we have heard, what we have seen with our eyes, what we have looked at and touched with our hands, concerning the word of life—this life was revealed, and we have seen it and testify to it, and declare to you the eternal life that was with the Father and was revealed to us—we declare to you what we have seen and heard so that you also may have fellowship with us; and truly our fellowship is with the Father and with his Son Jesus Christ. (1 John 1:1-3)

Implicit in this "declaration" is the invitation to come and see and believe. The faith to which readers are summoned in this passage is beyond the acceptance of specific beliefs—although it certainly includes that—and encompasses a living relationship with the living Lord.

The challenge before us now is to transpose this rich and nuanced biblical pattern of evangelization into our own context today. How exactly do we make our proclamation by inviting people—beginning with ourselves as a continuously evangelized community—to come and see, to meet and know the living Christ, the person of Jesus, and to become a part of his community of disciples who are related to him and to each other by bonds of faith?

Let's begin by anticipating what others suspect when we say that we want to evangelize them. When our contemporaries in this secular age hear that someone wants to evangelize them, they steel themselves for an unpleasant encounter. They have expectations of what will come their way. They expect, for example, an ideology or a completely prepackaged conceptual framework that describes the world and how they ought to live their lives. They may also expect to be pushed to affiliate with some form of institutional life, in other words, to join a religion with its various and multiple rituals and precepts. Finally, they no doubt wait for an onerous and freedom-denying moral code to be imposed upon them.

These are not unreasonable suspicions. Historically, secularity has meant emancipation from imposed ideologies, forced institutional life and religious observances, and an extrinsic moral code. With its focus on individuals, their self-expression, their freedom, and their capacity to create and direct their own lives and the world itself, secularity seems to stand in complete antithesis to the process and goals of evangelization—at least, in the minds and hearts of our thoroughgoing secular contemporaries. And here is the great surprise—the enormous variance between secular expectations of evangelization and the actual reality of evangelization as we have begun to understand it.

Evangelization that offers the invitation *Come and see* has a person, not a set of ideas, at the center of its concern. There is also something more immediate and more human about this evangelization that Pope Francis describes as "a mother with an open heart" than an ideology or philosophy of life might offer (*Evangelii Gaudium* 46–49). And far from the grim prospects of a rigid institutional life and its accompanying rigid moral codes, this evangelization brings an engaging joyfulness along with a continuously unfolding creative novelty (ibid. 2–8). These surprising turns are consequences of an evangelization that centers on the essential—the proclamation and introduction of the person of the living Christ whom we are to meet and see. Indeed, the element of surprise, which is not usually considered a dimension of church ministry, plays a decisive if unappreciated role in the gospels. What Jesus says, how he presents himself, what he does, and where and with whom he travels—these are all surprising, unexpected, and sometimes jarring realities for those whom he encounters. The element of surprise shook the assumptions and prejudices of those whom Jesus addressed. Similarly, surprise can break through today's encrustations of secularity, indifference, and absorption in the ordinary affairs of daily life.

Now we can raise important practical questions about how we can evangelize and be evangelized. How, for example, do we present the person of the living Christ and not simply a message about him to the world? How do we surprise people—and ourselves—in such a way that they must take a second look at their assumptions? I cannot claim definitive answers to these critical questions. I can only offer some suggestions that are possible ways to communicate the person of Jesus Christ and do so in a way that might surprise listeners.

I suggest offering four different kinds of invitations that specify the *Come and see* of the gospel. As I name the invitations, I will not list them in any particular order. And it is important to note that not all four invitations need to be offered. What does characterize each invitation in a surprising or unexpected way is the call to some immediate engagement with Jesus Christ. In other words, rather than explaining who Jesus is and then calling people to consider him, the invitations are given to meet him directly or to encounter him in various ways as a prelude to deciding whether and how we will put our faith in him. Finally, notice that these invitations are extended both to those who have not heard of him or known him as well as to the community of faith that is continuously being evangelized.

The first invitation is to *oratio-contemplatio*, to pray before him or to contemplate him. It may seem strange to evangelize by first calling people to pray to Jesus, but there is a precedent for this in the gospels. In Matthew's gospel (8:5-13; parallels in Luke 7:1-10 and John 4:46-54), a Roman centurion, who stands outside the faith of Israel, has his initial encounter with Jesus that begins with a prayer for help and ends with a confirmation of his faith. "When he entered Capernaum, a centurion came to him, appealing to him and saying, 'Lord, my servant is lying at home paralyzed, in terrible distress'" (Matt 8:5-6). The confidence this man places in Jesus, a confidence expressed in his prayer-request addressed to Jesus, leads Jesus to a confirmation of his faith: "Truly I tell you, in no one in Israel have I found such faith" (Matt 8:10).

A similar passage in Matthew (15:21-28; parallel in Mark 7:24-30) recounts the coming to "great faith" of a Canaanite woman. Like the Roman centurion, as a Canaanite, she stands outside the tradition of faith. She begins her encounter with Jesus with a desperate prayer-plea for her daughter: "Have mercy on me, Lord, Son of David; my daughter is tormented by a demon" (Matt 15:22). Jesus manifests reluctance to answer her request, but his reluctance only intensifies her pleading. Through her prayer and pleading, the Canaanite woman has met Jesus and come to faith in him.

The prelude to the prayers of the Roman centurion and the Canaanite woman was, no doubt, seeing Jesus, some contemplation of him even if from afar. In that contemplation, they saw his power, his kindness, and his capacity to heal and restore. Having contemplated his human compassion, his connection with the poor and suffering, and his capacity to transform broken lives, both the centurion and the woman are led to plead their case before him. In this process of *oratio-contemplatio*, they meet him, they see him, and they come to faith in him.

I suspect that our experiences in this secular age make us reluctant to begin our efforts of evangelization by first inviting people to *oratio-contemplatio*. It seems counterintuitive to begin with prayer. Doesn't it seem to make more sense logically to begin with why people should consider Jesus? And then, once they are solid in their faith, to invite them to prayer? In fact, the logic of the Gospel breaks our preconceptions of what makes for an orderly approach to evangelization. Moving people (including ourselves) to direct contact in *oratio-contemplatio* with Jesus brings us to the person of the living Lord and fulfills the invitation to come and see and believe. And ushering in the person of Jesus is exactly what we have come to understand as central to the proclamation that is evangelization.

The second invitation is to *lectio*, literally, reading. The usual expression in the spiritual tradition is *lectio divina* or holy reading. It refers to the slow and meditative reading of Sacred Scripture. Unlike most of our reading, which is directed to gathering information or being entertained, *lectio* becomes an experience of loving communication, much like reading a letter sent by a very dear friend or a spouse. In that kind of communication, details of information assume a secondary position to the living connection that is established between persons who care very much for each other.

The evangelizing invitation to *lectio* means introducing people to the teachings of Jesus contained in the gospels. In its best sense, *lectio* does not refer to bits and pieces of interesting information. Done properly, it effects a connection with Jesus, who communicates with readers and listeners through the text. Again, while respecting the contents of the message, *lectio* moves the reader and listener beyond the message to connect with the one who is within it. In that sense, *lectio* becomes a means to present the living Christ by inviting people to come and see.

When people are adequately prepared for *lectio*, they will inevitably make surprising discoveries that lead to amazement. This is the case in Capernaum when Jesus teaches and heals. The crowd's response is, "They were all amazed, and they kept on asking one another, 'What is this? A new teaching—with authority!'" (Mark 1:27). The same response occurs on other occasions, for example, after responding to the question about paying taxes, Mark records, "And they were utterly amazed at him" (Mark 12:17).

Again, encouraging people, especially those who do not believe, to read the gospels seems a counterintuitive way to make them disciples. Won't they get stuck on questions of literal interpretation—did this really happen? Did Jesus really say this or do that? With proper direction to guide people to "hear" Jesus communicating in a personal way through and within the text, it is possible to make *lectio* an effective means of introducing him as a living person. Once Jesus is introduced through the gospels, he can meet those who are willing to listen. He can teach and explain the meaning of the coming of the reign of God, the call to repentance, the possibility of healing, the way of compassionate living, and the hope and promise of eternal life.

A third form of invitation—to come and see—is the invitation to share in *diakonia*, the service that characterizes the entire life and mission of Jesus. He defines his purpose in Mark's gospel: "For the Son of Man came not to be served but to serve, and to give his life as a ransom for many" (Mark 10:45). A very practical way of encountering Jesus is by joining in works of service, justice, and charity.

Again, it may seem counterintuitive to proclaim Jesus by inviting those who have not yet found faith in him to participate in actions that involve him or are accomplished in his name. Practically, this proclamation can look like bringing people along to feed the hungry, shelter the homeless, visit the sick and imprisoned, and comfort those who carry life's heavy burdens. Why do this? Because we have the very good word of Jesus when he describes the judgment of the nations that when we give a drink to those who are thirsty or welcome the stranger among us or care for the sick, we are encountering him. "Truly I tell you, just as you did it to one of the least of these who are members of my family, you did it to me" (Matt 25:40).

The *diakonia* or service in which and through which we can meet Jesus also extends to embrace larger social concerns. Upholding justice and doing so systemically, for example, is a powerful example of service that proclaims Jesus. The 1971 synodal document Justice in the World states unambiguously, "Action on behalf of justice and participation in the transformation of the world fully appear to us as a constitutive dimension of the preaching of the Gospel, or, in other words, of the Church's mission for the redemption of the human race and its liberation from every oppressive situation."[7] And beyond working for justice, our involvement in works of forgiveness, reconciliation, peacemaking, care for the environment, and healing brings us and whoever would engage these works in direct contact with the living Christ.[8] This is evident in a powerful passage from the Letter to the Ephesians: "For he is our peace; in his flesh he has made both groups into one and has broken down the dividing wall, that is, the hostility between us" (Eph 2:14).

For people of a more practical bent—as so many Americans are—this kind of direct action and engagement is a very appropriate way to introduce people to Jesus. We bring people (and ourselves, of course) to meet him and know him in doing for others what he did

---

[7] Synod of Bishops, Justice in the World, introduction, November 30, 1971.

[8] See, for example, Pontifical Council for Justice and Peace, Compendium of the Social Doctrine of the Church, "Evangelization and Social Doctrine," 60–71 (Vatican City State: Libreria Editrice Vaticana, 2004). And see *Laudato Sì*, "The Gospel of Creation," 62–100.

for them. We also come to know him in the faces of those whom we serve, because he assured us of his presence in them. In other words, we evangelize and are evangelized in Jesus' actions, which are deeds of mercy, justice, and peacemaking that become a powerful proclamation and clear introduction of him who invites us to faith. Our participation in his *diakonia* is a portal for going to see him and stay with him.

A fourth and final means of proclamation is to invite others (and reinvite ourselves) to share in Christ's *koinonia*, his communion and community. He dwells, as St. Paul never tires of saying, in the community, which is his body. He says, for example, "Now you are the body of Christ and individually members of it" (1 Cor 12:27). And individuals can participate in a living communion with him who is their hope. Paul writes to the Colossians, "To them God chose to make known how great among the Gentiles are the riches of the glory of this mystery, which is *Christ in you, the hope of glory*" (Col 1:27, emphasis added).

If Christ dwells and is to be met in the community of his follow-ers and their communal life, then how do we invite those outside of the community to join in? Very simply, we ask them to be with us. In other words, we ask them to be with us as we listen to God's word, as we lift our prayers together to God, as we struggle to live well together, and as we take up the responsibilities entrusted to our care. Again, it may seem strange and surprising to invite people who do not yet believe to participate in the life of a community of faith. In fact, that invitation to share in the life of the community says, "Come and see." The presence of the living Christ becomes palpable to those who hear the voice of his followers, see their faces at prayer, and watch them praising and thanking God in worship. Those who stand outside of faith cannot fully participate in the *koinonia*, but they can come and see and perhaps move toward faith because of that encounter.

Of course, this avenue of proclamation by bringing people into the life of the community will inevitably have its awkward moments. And those who come may be very tentative. In fact, this kind of proc-lamation that invites those who do not yet believe to come into the community or *koinonia* may be so awkward that it would not seem to have a biblical foundation. In fact, we do not frequently encounter this approach in the New Testament and for good reason. The communities were small and often fragile and frequently even under siege. They could only be sustained by people who had clearly made a firm commitment. The indiscriminate participation of outsiders could easily have damaged the ecology of these early communities of faith. At the same time, bringing those who do not yet believe into the life of the believing community was not entirely absent. It is evident, for example, in Paul's experience with the Corinthian community. That community, so gifted and so eclectic, had an openness that enabled outsiders to come inside to experience what Paul called the Body of Christ in the community. Those outside of faith could be brought inside to hear the invitation to come and see.

An example of outsiders coming inside the community appears in Paul's reflections on the gifts of tongues and prophecy in the Corinthian community. Notice the path to faith that comes through a direct participation in the *koinonia* or community of faith as Paul describes it:

> Tongues, then, are a sign not for believers but for unbelievers, while prophecy is not for unbelievers but for believers. If, therefore, the whole church comes together and all speak in tongues, *and outsiders or unbelievers enter*, will they not say that you are out of your mind? But if all prophesy, an unbeliever or outsider who enters is reproved by all and called to account by all. After the secrets of the unbeliever's heart are disclosed, that person will bow down before God and worship him, declaring, "God is really among you." (1 Cor 14:22-25, emphasis added)

Paul seems to be saying, "Let them see who you are in Christ by the power of the Holy Spirit. Let them see themselves. And if this happens, they may well come to faith and become one with us."

The four surprising and counterintuitive strategies of *oratio-contemplatio*, *lectio*, *diakonia*, and *koinonia* are an approach to proclaiming the living Christ by inviting those outside the family of faith to come and see. There may be other strategies, but these seem especially strong and well-anchored in the biblical tradition. Additionally, each one of these strategies is not meant solely for nonbelievers who are summoned to faith in Jesus Christ. Each one of these strategies is part of the ongoing life of believers in the believing community. That community evangelizes and is both continuously and simultaneously evangelized.

Practical questions remain. How do we effectively implement these strategies? How do we bring ourselves and others who are not part of our believing community into *oratio-contemplatio, lectio, diakonia,* and *koinonia*? I leave it to people directly engaged in pastoral ministry to explore and identify the specifics of implementation. At some point, however, they will probably need to provide "scripts" or sample conversations that help those in the church overcome their reticence and graciously invite people to come and see.

We have considered the first and foundational question: *What are you looking for?* The final response to that question, when all our options are explored and all our possibilities are exhausted, is Jesus Christ. We who believe have come to recognize and know that whatever we are looking for or think that we are looking for will have no point of complete satisfaction until it embraces the mystery of Jesus Christ. The challenge for believers is to bring those who do not believe to Jesus. This fundamental challenge of evangelization includes the proclamation of the good news about Jesus Christ and, even more decisively, the introduction of the person of the living Christ so that people may come to him, see him, and believe in him. And here we have explored the great invitation that belongs to John's gospel: come and see. To concretize that invitation, we considered the four strategies of *oratio-contemplatio, lectio, diakonia,* and *koinonia*. This reflection now enables us to move to the next great question of the gospel: *Are you going to stay?*

Are You Going to Stay? (See John 6:67)

After the Bread of Life discourse, John reports that "many of his disciples turned back and no longer went about with him" (John 6:66). With that clear fact so evident, John adds, "So Jesus asked the twelve, 'Do you also wish to go away?'" (John 6:67). We can take that question and accurately transpose it in a positive direction: *Are you going to stay?* This becomes the crucial question of decision and commitment, essential elements for an evangelized and evangelizing community. Simply from a human perspective, any intentional community—and such is the evangelized and evangelizing community of faith—depends for its very survival on the commitment of those who belong to it.[9]

Although commitment is absolutely necessary for the formation of an intentional community, it is a complex experience that is often freighted with difficulties, especially in today's climate. We will explore the challenge and essential elements of commitment in several steps. A biblical context for commitment from St. Paul will introduce the theme for us. Then, we will consider the threefold dimension of acceptance, decision, and commitment itself. Finally, we will identify the particular difficulties surrounding commitment in our secular age and how we might practically respond to those difficulties and challenges in light of our biblical tradition.

When it is a matter of faith and attachment to Jesus Christ, St. Paul is completely decisive, and he expects the communities of faith that he founded to be equally decisive in their faith commitments. A clear instance of Paul's insistence on full, clear, and decisive commitment in faith can be found in his Second Letter to the Corinthians:

> Do I make my plans according to ordinary human standards, ready to say "Yes, yes" and "No, no" at the same time? As surely as God is faithful, our word to you has not been "Yes and No." For the Son of God, Jesus Christ, whom we proclaimed among you, Silvanus and Timothy and I, was not "Yes and No"; but in him it is always "Yes." For in him every one of God's promises is a "Yes." For this reason it is through him that we say the "Amen," to the glory of God. But it is God who establishes us with you in Christ and has anointed us, by putting his seal on us and giving us his Spirit in our hearts as a first installment. (2 Cor 1:17-22)

Notice in Paul's words the levels of firm and faithful commitment: (1) God is firmly committed to his promises; (2) Jesus is firmly

---

[9] For a sociological perspective, see Rosabeth Moss Kanter, *Commitment and Community: Communes and Utopias in Sociological Perspective* (Cambridge, MA: Harvard University Press, 1972).

committed in his "Yes"; (3) Paul is firmly committed in his proclamation of Jesus Christ; (4) the community stands firm in its commitment by voicing its "Amen." In Paul's estimation, there is no
room for hesitation or vacillation, because God in Jesus Christ has
set the pattern for us. An evangelized and evangelizing community,
therefore, cannot step away from its own firm commitments nor
from summoning others to make similar commitments. With this
perspective from Paul, we can now consider the nature and process
of a faith commitment in more detail.

The full faith commitment of disciples builds on two prior steps,
and they are acceptance and decision. After responding to the invitation to come and see Jesus, a person is called to accept or receive
Jesus as alive and real. More specifically, this means accepting him
as the living Christ who is present in the church, in the sacraments,
in the liturgical worship of the community, in the church's service
especially to the poor, and in the church's teaching that conveys
Christ's own message. This sense of acceptance characterizes the
response of the Samaritans of the town of Sychar who were introduced to Jesus by a woman of the town who had gone to draw water
at the well where Jesus was. After the woman's witness to Jesus,
the townspeople found themselves in direct contact with him. They
signaled their acceptance of him with these words to the woman: "It
is no longer because of what you said that we believe, for we have
heard for ourselves, and we know that this is truly the Savior of the
world" (John 3:42).

Beyond accepting Jesus, those who would follow him are called to
something more. They are summoned to make a decision to follow
him and to belong to him as his disciples. Deciding can be stretched
out across a period of time, or it can happen quickly. In the case of
the call of Matthew, for example, everything moves with a rapid
pace. Everything essential happens in one verse. Matthew makes a
life-changing decision in short order: "As Jesus was walking along,
he saw a man called Matthew sitting at the tax booth; and he said
to him, 'Follow me.' And he got up and followed him" (Matt 9:9).
Similarly, a group of fishermen hear Jesus' call, and St. Luke says,
"When they had brought their boats to shore, they left everything
and followed him" (Luke 5:11). Although the sweeping decision to

follow Jesus moves quickly, presumably they had in some way come to him, seen him, known him, accepted him, and then decided to follow him. What is especially striking about these decisions is deliberateness. Each decision is evidently a very intentional act. It must be so, because those who follow Jesus in the gospels leave everything behind. They detach themselves from a previous way of life to follow him. That detachment leads to the final movement of commitment.

Commitment to Jesus Christ as his believing disciples, in the end, is only possible because of a committed attachment to him. And this attachment is an intimate sharing of life comparable, in the words of Jesus, to the relationship between the vine and the branches (see John 15:1-11). This attachment has its necessary foundations or conditions in the movements that we have already identified: coming to him, knowing him, accepting him, deciding for him, and now attaching oneself wholeheartedly to him. In fact, this union is so close that the disciple bears the very presence of the Lord in the world: "Very truly, I tell you, whoever receives one whom I send receives me, and whoever receives me receives him who sent me" (John 13:20).

If we are to be evangelized and if we are to evangelize, then we need to have a clear sense of how commitments are made or not made today. In other words, as clear as the biblical patterns for commitment are, they don't matter if our contemporaries—and perhaps we ourselves—are unable to embrace them or embrace them with great difficulty. What is our context for commitment in this secular age now and for the foreseeable future?

We and our contemporaries hear Jesus' question, "Are you going to stay?" An unsurprising response might be, "I'm not sure." When people in a secular age are called to a commitment, they frequently hesitate. Because truth seems fluid and even unstable, because so many people are so aware of their vulnerability and therefore become risk-adverse, because anything like a significant commitment that is a long-term or totally enveloping reality seems so foreign in our culture—for these reasons and many others, people living now and for the foreseeable future will have difficulty making commitments. Clearly, this is not a difficulty restricted to matters of faith and religion. Commitments today do not come easy for marriage or parenting or employment. The irony in this secular age is that despite its exultation of freedom and personal choice, individuals are often frozen or paralyzed when it comes time to make a decision or to make a commitment.

The call to a faith commitment is especially fraught with difficulty for all the reasons that we identified earlier. There are the inevitable suspicions about whatever cannot be empirically verified. Additionally, there are suspicions that personal freedom is surrendered in making a faith commitment. And, of course, suspicions abound about the workings of institutional religion that is, for many, equivalent to faith. These difficulties certainly affect those who are to be evangelized, but they also leave an imprint on those who do the evangelization. Remember that the faith community is both evangelized and evangelizing. And that faith community itself lives immersed in the culture that gives rise to all the difficulties that people have in making commitments. So, in its own way, the community of faith must also face this context of difficulties in its process of continuously being evangelized even as it evangelizes others.

How is it possible to cut through the difficulties and bring people to acceptance, decision, and, finally, committed attachment to faith in Jesus Christ lived out in his community of disciples? In responding to this extraordinarily important question, we need to be clear about what is *not* a good direction, at the same time that we offer some positive possibilities. So, it is not a good thing to evangelize hesitantly and so try to accommodate all the difficulties that people might sense. Our evangelizing others and ourselves ought not to go forward with hesitation but with directness, even that bold and forthright speech (*parrhesia*) that Paul uses to characterize his approach. This is also the directness of Jesus in the gospels who says quite clearly and in unadorned fashion, "Follow me."

Our efforts of evangelization ought not to diminish the demands of following Jesus as his committed and believing disciples, in order to make the choice for discipleship easier and more attractive by the standards of conventional wisdom. In fact, as we evangelize, we should prominently display the demands and challenges of the Gospel. In fact, we ought to push forward the heroic dimensions of the Christian life that far exceed the expectations of conventional religiosity that most people have. The dramatic instance of martyrs across the ages and in our own time can underscore what is at stake when we fully commit ourselves in faith and attachment to Jesus Christ in his church. The stories of saints' unbounded charity to those in need can also illustrate the dramatic stakes of a fully dedicated life as a disciple of Jesus.

Finally, when we evangelize, we ought not to deliver our message and the very person of Jesus and then walk away, as if we had now completed a task given to us. If we walk away after "doing our thing," we are effectively abandoning the people that we want to help bring to faith. Instead of leaving them or abandoning them, we dedicate ourselves to their accompaniment. We continue to walk with them, and so mediate—in our own way—the promise of Jesus, "And remember, I am with you always, to the end of the age" (Matt 28:20).

Directness, honest challenge, and generous accompaniment—these seem to be essential directions for evangelizing people who are moving toward faith. These are the people who have come, have seen, have accepted, and have decided. They make a final step of commitment by attaching themselves to Jesus and his community, the church. There may be other directions, but these seem to be essential as we help people unfold Jesus' great question of commitment: *Are you going to stay?*

Go and Proclaim the Good News (See Mark 16:15)

The fourth and final moment in the process of evangelization is the invitation *Go and proclaim the Good News.* What began as the question of human searching and longing that led to introducing Jesus (come and see) that, in turn, led to decision and commitment—all this now culminates in mission, a sending out with purpose. This brings us full circle and reiterates a fundamental conviction. There is a reciprocal and mutual relationship between evangelizing and being evangelized and, vice versa, between being evangelized and evangelizing. They are inseparable dimensions of a single and unitary movement of the Gospel being brought to life in the world. Pope Francis speaks of this movement in terms of "missionary disciples":

> In virtue of their baptism, all the members of the People of God have become missionary disciples (cf. Mt 28:19). All the baptized, whatever their position in the Church or their level of instruction in the faith, are agents of evangelization . . . The new evangelization calls for personal involvement on the part of each of the baptized. Every Christian is challenged, here and now, to be actively engaged in evangelization; indeed, anyone who has truly experienced God's saving love does not need much time or lengthy training to go out and proclaim that love. Every Christian is a missionary to the extent that he or she has encountered the love of God in Christ Jesus: we no longer say that we are "disciples" and "missionaries," but rather that we are always "missionary disciples." If we are not convinced, let us look at those first disciples, who, immediately after encountering the gaze of Jesus, went forth to proclaim him joyfully: "We have found the Messiah!" (Jn 1:41). (*Evangelii Gaudium* 120)

It may be helpful at this point to contrast evangelization as we have considered it with the dynamics of the secular culture and age in which we live and in which the Gospel is proclaimed. The dynamism of our secular age, as we have seen, consists in a received and then communicated message about the sufficiency of human reason, the ideal of free self-determination, the standard of toleration for all things except for intolerance, the primacy of subjective experience, and the inevitability of finding not one stable truth but many truths of relative value to each other. These convictions serve as a kind of received secular wisdom that then finds expression in the "rich cultural productions" that sustain and promote the ideas of the secular age. In other words, secularity, especially in its closed-ended form, is a received ideology that underwrites a consistent and often seemingly rigid pattern for our living together. The way of the Gospel, the way of evangelization, is much different.

With evangelization as we have understood it, the Gospel becomes a generative force for our lives individually and our life together. Unlike the closed-ended secular convictions that coalesce into an ideology, evangelization and the Gospel it proclaims are not about ideas but about a person. Unlike the received wisdom of secularity, the Gospel is both received and then also given. This is clearly indicated in Matthew's gospel in the great missionary discourse of chapter 10: "You received without payment; give without payment" (Matt 10:8). Unlike the secular penchant to organize and interpret life in a fixed set of categories, the Gospel not only organizes and interprets life but also creates new possibilities for life. These new possibilities crash through the limits and barriers imposed by sin, death, physical limitation, and various forms of malice both human and other. The Gospel can then create and sustain new life through forgiveness, eternal life, and new forms of justice, reconciliation, and ways of living together.

The Gospel proclaimed in evangelization does not compete with secular ideology. Rather, it transcends what clearly emerges as the narrow confines of secularity. The Gospel brings newness and creativity to life.

Those who come, see, and meet Jesus and then accept him and attach themselves to him inevitably cannot contain their discovery. The mission of communicating him to others wells up within and then finds expression when the first opportunity presents itself. This is what happened for the Samaritan woman at the well. After her encounter with Jesus, the gospel says, "Then the woman left her water jar and went back to the city. She said to the people, 'Come and see a man who told me everything I have ever done! He cannot be the Messiah, can he?'" (John 4:28-29). Notice the link with the earlier invitation that Jesus extends to the two disciples of John the Baptist who were following him: "Come and see" (John 1:39). It is the very same invitation that Philip extends to Nathanael: "Come and see" (John 1:46). Once discovered, Jesus cannot remain hidden by his disciples. They will necessarily go out and engage others in the very same process that brought them to faith in the living Christ. And so the circular and generative movement of being evangelized and evangelizing continues forward.

Concluding Reflection

We began our reflections by trying to anticipate the future of faith, religion, and the church. The perspectives of philosophy, history, cultural analysis, and sociology suggest a diminished future, if current trends continue. These prospects sadden and discourage believers who have come to know and deeply value their faith. They understand the great good of faith, religion, and the church. And quite naturally, they desire to do something that would change the current course. The questions are, What exactly can we do? What ought we to do? With a focus on the church and faith, some options became immediately clear. The first was to do nothing new but rather to let things move on their current trajectory. This strategy, which is really a non-strategy, seemed unacceptable. The second was to accept the fewer number of believers who participate in the life of the church and who try to live out their faith in daily life. Even more than accepting the smaller church, this second strategy fosters the development of a more compact and more committed community. Although this choice with its emphasis on genuine faith and commitment has its attractions, it also risks sliding into an unacceptable elitism. In addition, it risks abandoning the inclusive call of the Gospel for the sake of a purer and more genuine community of faith. Dissatisfaction with these two strategies led us to consider a third possibility.

The third response brought us to a renewed experience of evangelization. There are distinctive and specifying features of evangelization as we considered it. In the first place, it is essential to understand that the community engaged in evangelizing is itself in a continuous process of being evangelized. Pope Francis spoke of this binary relationship by identifying believers as missionary disciples. They are evangelizing missionaries, but, at the same time, they are disciples who are continuously being evangelized.

A second distinctive and essential dimension of this evangelization is its personal character. Evangelization is synonymous with preaching a message. And that is true. Even more, however, inside of the message is the presentation of a person, the living Christ. That means that the goal of evangelization is not only embracing the truth of a message or an idea but also engaging in a relationship with Jesus. In this movement toward relationship with Jesus Christ and with each other in him, we follow an important pattern in the Bible that includes two questions and two invitations: *What are you looking for? Come and see. Are you going to stay? Go and proclaim the Good News.*

The first question—*What are you looking for?*—captured the searching that characterizes our lives, as we look for fulfillment or something beyond ourselves. It is this question that leads to the invitation that follows: *Come and see.* This is the introduction to Jesus Christ. And as we described it, this introduction can take some very direct forms, such as prayer, exposure to the gospels, participation in the service of charity and compassion for others, and participation in the life of a believing community. The second question follows: *Are you going to stay?* This question calls people to accept Jesus, to decide for him, and then to make a commitment of attachment to him. Finally, the second invitation is *Go and proclaim the Good News.* This, in a sense, closes the circle. To be evangelized, that is, to be joined in relationship with the living Christ, inevitably leads us to evangelize others. We bring to others the one we have found and believed. We start and end as missionary disciples.

With this model of evangelization, the church assumes a particular shape. It is the church of the question, of the possibility, of the decision, and of the mission. And in this, the church does not look like a self-absorbed institution that is bent on its own survival. The church really emerges as a servant of both God and humanity, striving to be true to the word of life implanted by the Lord and striving to serve that same word of life in the lives of real people.

So, in the end, what happens with the secular culture, the secular age, that began these reflections? It remains the context of this world, at least the world of the North Atlantic. And it is not an entirely bad context, on the condition that it does not become absolutist and closed in on itself. Eventually, it must honestly reckon with its own insufficiency. Otherwise, it will become absolutist and closed in on itself.

Will the evangelization that we have considered reshape the secular culture? I don't know. Will this evangelization increase the numbers of people who participate in the life of the church? That, too, is uncertain. Will this evangelization at least have some impact on the world for the world's transformation? I certainly hope so, but I also don't know if that will be the case and, if so, in what measure. With all the uncertainty about results, what, then, is the point?

If we cannot be confident about the results of our efforts, we can be confident in God who has entrusted his word, his Son, and his life to us. We can echo Paul's words to his beloved Philippian community: "I am confident of this, that the one who began a good work among you will bring it to completion by the day of Jesus Christ" (Phil 1:6). The point—to echo the thoughts of Saint Teresa of Calcutta—is not to develop a formula for our success but rather to find a path that keeps us faithful to what God wants. In our complicated and challenging secular age, we can begin to take steps in that direction.

Afterword

The Chicago Experience
of "Renew My Church"

Cardinal Blase J. Cupich

I n the first part of his reflections, Fr. Cameli identifies certain important cultural and social markers for the church's life, especially in North America. We live in an increasingly secular environment. Fewer people participate in the life of the church, and the trajectory of younger people, who often have a very limited grasp of faith, indicates a continuing trend of diminished participation. These markers do not simply reflect an analytical academic exercise. The lives of real people wrap around these trends, and I can personally attest to that. Our response to the future, a future to which God summons, involves more than ideas. We are the inheritors of a great tradition of faith that has found embodiment in visible structures and institutional life. Our renewal must take into account the complexity of our situation.

As the archbishop of Chicago, I am called to be a pastor to a large and very diverse population of Catholics who are subject to the trends that Fr. Cameli notes. Additionally, in Chicago, we have inherited infrastructure that, in many instances, was built to meet the needs of people who are now long gone and have been replaced by very different populations. Moreover, these parishes operated within an environment of social cohesion that supported communal life. That environment in many cases no longer exists. Thus, the principal challenges are both internal-spiritual (how to revitalize the faith and spiritual life of people) and external-organizational (how to manage structures that are no longer up to the task of serving people well).

These facts and challenges impel us to action, although the exact shape of that action continues to emerge with greater clarity as we move forward. Certainly, as we have identified them, the prospects for the future are challenging. Still, they are not entirely bleak. Many good people do participate in the life of the church. Faith is central to their lives, and they want to share that faith with others, especially those closest to them. Our own faith also speaks to us of the encouraging presence of the Holy Spirit, who always accompanies us in the church. We find encouragement in the words and example of Pope Francis. He urges us not only to go out to the world, which is in so much need of the Gospel, but also to do so together as a synodal church discerning the movement of the Spirit.

Earlier, Fr. Cameli suggested three possible directions when we face these social, cultural, and religious challenges: do nothing, plan to shrink, or reengage the church as a community that is evangelized and, simultaneously, evangelizing. In the Archdiocese of Chicago, we are pursuing this third and final direction but in a way that also takes into account our complex situation that includes both spiritual concerns and concerns about physical plants, financial outlooks, and projected availability of personnel, especially ordained priests. The process has been named "Renew My Church," a title inspired by an early experience of St. Francis of Assisi in the church of San Damiano. There are many reasons for drawing inspiration for our own process of renewal from the experience of St. Francis. The most compelling reason, in my mind, is that Jesus' words to Francis ignited a powerful movement of new evangelization, a reclaiming of the power of the Gospel in people's lives.

Permit me now to cite reflections that I offered to the priests of the archdiocese at the very beginning of our process in September 2015. These words will help to explain the evangelized-evangelizing dynamic of "Renew My Church" in the Archdiocese of Chicago. They also set a proper context for the aspects of material planning, which I will explain later.

From the Address of Archbishop Cupich
to the Presbyteral Assembly on September 29, 2015

It occurs to me that as we take up the new initiative being presented today ["Renew My Church"], we need something to keep our focus throughout this process. I want to return to that first moment of the call of Francis. You know the story. Praying in front of the now famous San Damiano crucifix, the little Umbrian friar heard Christ call out to him in an era of great turmoil for the church: "Francis, Francis, go and repair my Church which, as you can see, is falling into ruins." He came to understand, as should we, that Christ was calling him to much more than the renovation of a dilapidated building. Yes, there are structural and organizational implications for the tasks before us, but such work always has to be centered and balanced by the question how will this lead to a spiritual renewal of the people we serve, how will this reinvigorate our mission and, yes, how will it keep us as a presbyterate true to the calling we have received to be servant leaders?

So, let me propose to you that beginning today and throughout this process, we use as a kind of touchstone the now famous crucifix of San Damiano. Today I want to begin a meditation on that scene, which I invite you to add to in the coming weeks and months, by pointing out this morning three aspects of that icon which strike me as important for keeping in focus our task going forward.

First, notice that the crucified Christ is very much alive and poised to speak to us. It is important to recall that the icon, as an art form, is unique for it portrays the holy one imaged as the subject, who acts. The world does not gaze on it, but instead is the object of its gaze; the world lives in the gaze of the holy one. Only with the Renaissance were these roles reversed and the world became the subject looking at those imaged as passive objects. For me, this suggests that we have to remember that what we are doing is first Christ's work not ours. That is our reference point, and not the world's expectations of success. Also, notice that Christ is drawing our attention to higher things, as we glance upward. Christ, who Pope Francis reminds us in the *Joy of the Gospel*, is the risen one, who is always doing something new. We should not be afraid to raise our sights and consider new, creative and imaginative ways of doing things. We should be emboldened by the conviction that this is a graced time. We all fall into the trap of letting the daily grind of tasks, the failures and disappointments that bring public humiliation and institutional degradation for us to lose perspective and to eclipse that we are living in a graced time.

Yes, it is true, the so-called glory days of *Going My Way* are passed, the enticing nectar of secularism runs deep in the veins of our people and perhaps each one of us, and we seemed to be beleaguered as we face shrinking communities, few human and financial resources, mounting legal costs, and less respect in the public square for our teachings. We can allow all of this to eclipse the reality of this very special moment in history. But, brothers as I reflect on my forty years as a priest I am thrilled to live in these days, which I find filled with God's manifold works in a Church willing to be led not by our successes or gains but by the Spirit of the Risen Christ. He is the actor in history. In fact, don't we know this personally as we reflect on our own calling to the priesthood? The one who calls the church to something new is the same one who called us.

And just as Christ is the actor, so too must we see ourselves, his body as actors in the world. This, at the least means for us in this moment, not reducing the church to an object, an institution that we have to maintain, a business defined by a bottom line, but as Pope Francis has urged, an agent which runs a field hospital. All of us, members of the church, must see ourselves as that agent, not living for themselves, as a self-referential Church, a social enclave, but one that goes out, invites, serves, heals. Again, for us as a presbyterate to communicate all of that to our people, maybe each one of us needs to personally return to the moment we were called, when we each received our vocation, remembering that it was not we who chose him but he who chose us.

The second thing that draws my attention is that Christ is depicted in this icon as both dying and rising. Notice that just above the crucified one is a scene of Jesus in heaven with the Father, surrounded by angels. The work ahead of us will make demands and involve sacrifices, just as it did for those immigrants who came before us and who built the church blessing us today. What we begin today, will involve sacrifice, a kind of dying. The dying that comes in leaving behind the false comforts of working in isolation, or the dying involved in unmasking the illusion that we can continue to ignore hard facts about limited resources. Let's be honest, there is a dying already going on. We see it in the slow yet progressive deterioration of the size of our communities with demographic and other changes, in the mounting deferred capital maintenance of our buildings, in the shrinking of our presbyterate and the religious communities who have blessed us.

There is a dying going on already, but what we are called to is a dying that leads to resurrection. Fundamentally, our task in all of this is not to brace our people for the dying and sacrifice, but to rekindle in them a belief in the resurrection. We have to instill in them throughout this process the hopeful vision that we are going to be a more vibrant, alive, vital and life-giving Church in the dying and sacrifice. That surely motivated our immigrant ancestors who came here. They boldly took on the sacrifices because they believed new life would come from it for themselves and others who would follow. . . .

Finally, notice all the figures in the scene. At Christ's right are Mary and John, whom he gave to each other as mother and son. But there is more. There is the new family of God in the figures on the other side. Mary Magdalene, Mary the mother of James, and the unnamed centurion whose servant was cured and his whole household became disciples. The servant is peeking over the head of the centurion. Also, at the bottom are Longinus and Stephaton, soldiers who participated in the crucifixion. All this suggests that our aim in all we do is to renew the church by making it a family of families, a family that supports other families. All are to be included, people on the margins, even those who are guilty and yet part of the history of salvation. It is about building a new solidarity and not leaving anyone behind. Our world needs and thirsts for this. Is not the fulsome enthusiastic response to the Pope by the world a vivid sign of the deep aspirations in the human family for an end to exclusion and a great unity in the human family?

Again, I offer all of this just as a start and an invitation . . .

The Renewal of Parish and Archdiocesan Structures

These reflections offered to the priests at the end of September 2015 underscore the heart of the process of "Renew My Church." It truly is a process of spiritual renewal and revitalization. That process unfolds as individuals and communities reclaim both their identity (who they are) and their mission (what their purpose is). All this, of course, happens in the context of a church that is visible, structured, and institutionally embodied. So, as we move forward with "Renew My Church," we can neither one-sidedly "spiritualize" the process nor one-sidedly "materialize" it. Engaging both spiritual renewal and structural renewal, which serves to support the spiritual mission, entails an integral approach that balances and links both dimensions. I will consider that particular challenge shortly. For now, permit me to give a snapshot of the process of structural renewal.

The Archdiocese of Chicago benefited immensely from the generous services of the McKinsey consulting group. Representatives of McKinsey looked at the structural, financial, physical, and organizational aspects of the archdiocese and the parishes. They took into account the human dimension, especially the demographics of the archdiocese as well as the personnel in service to the mission, with a particular focus on the number of ordained priests now and projected into the future.

At this point (the summer of 2016), the structural plan based on data from McKinsey and a diocesan-wide listening and feedback process is still in the process of being more exactly formulated. Some elements, however, are already in place. Parish groupings are being established, so that conversations can begin and eventually lead to different leadership models, including parish closure or merger, a multisite single parish, a multiparish cluster, and independent but collaborative agreements among parishes. This restructuring must take into account the data of our annual October count, demographic analysis, mission vitality indicators, capital needs, operating stability, and geographical and cultural considerations. Spiritually, a given community in communion with the larger community also needs to engage a discernment process that seeks to identify where God is calling the community and its resources.

Discernment and Planning

Structural or organizational planning alone, as necessary as it is, cannot yield the kind of renewal that we hope for and need. Were it so, we could achieve renewal simply by a technical application of certain criteria and a rearrangement of our resources. In fact, true renewal follows a collective act of conversion, a turning again to the Lord and a renewed embrace of our identity and mission as God's church. Besides planning, this integral renewal requires discernment, an attentive watchfulness, and a reading of our situation and circumstances to identify the direction in which God is calling us.

Ultimately, this integral renewal will lead us to greater authenticity as an evangelized and an evangelizing church. We will then stand more secure in our identity as the community of Jesus' disciples and in our mission to bring him to the world. The great challenge, as I have seen it, is to hold to *both* planning *and* discernment before the church that embarks on the journey of renewal. Because it seems more accessible and because it is empirically verifiable, structural planning often becomes the default position. Discernment and spiritual renewal seem more elusive, and they tend to fade into the background. Both planning and discernment, however, are the necessary elements of renewal and moving into the future with grace and confidence.

Foundational Convictions

As we have begun this process of "Renew My Church" in the Archdiocese of Chicago, certain convictions have become clearer than ever to me. They are not original to our process, but they seem to be especially relevant, especially in today's social-cultural context as Fr. Cameli has described it.

God is with us. The Spirit leads us. The title of this book brings together church, faith, and future. In the end, whatever renewal we embrace will be a renewal of faith. If that is the end point, in some way it must also be the beginning and the sustaining force of our efforts. We believe that we are not alone in this enterprise and that the Lord is with us. We also believe that the Holy Spirit guides the church. If we allow the Spirit to prompt us, we will find our right direction.

We must pay attention to the facts—the particular situation and circumstances of our life together. We are a sacramental church.

Indeed, the beginning of the Second Vatican Council's Dogmatic Constitution on the Church says that the church is in the manner of a sacrament of the unity of all humanity in God. Sacrament means visible and tangible signs, that is, spiritual realities rooted in worldly realities. So, we can never afford to prescind from what the poet Gerard Manley Hopkins called the "thisness" of things. We cannot and must not hide in abstractions.

A renewed and renewing church is a synodal church. Pope Francis has set a pace for the entire church by reclaiming a significant element of the renewal ushered in by the Second Vatican Council. That council depended on "reading the signs of the times," in the words of Pope John XXIII. That, in turn, meant listening attentively to the experiences of people. A synodal church comes together in dialogue and communion, anticipating that the Spirit of God will move the hearts of gathered believers. If we listen, we will learn.

Renewal in the church will lead to the formation of adult believers. The goal of renewal in the church cannot be to make people more dependent on others for the direction of their lives. The exact opposite is true. Renewal, if it is genuine, will lead to the formation of adult believers. They will not be autonomous and separated from the community. In fact, a sign of their adulthood is participation in freedom in the life of the community. And they will be capable of making their own decisions, taking initiatives, and being responsive to the directions in which the Spirit prompts them.

A church that is fully alive is a church without fear and also without rancor. A church that draws its life from the faith of believers is a confident church. It may encounter difficulties and even forms of persecution, but it remains unafraid because it is convinced of God's presence. And even when the church encounters serious obstacles and even hostility, it does not assume a warrior stance. In segments of today's culture and social organization, there is a temptation for the church to sound a battle cry. In fact, if grounded in faith with a secure identity and sense of mission, the church will be serene in the face of a negative cultural environment. In a secular world, the church only needs to be itself. The church serves the world, even when the world is wary and reluctant in matters of faith. And the church provides, in the words of Pope Francis, a field hospital in the middle of a wounded world and a bruised humanity, in order to be a caring and healing presence.

An effective church in mission adapts to the world and its culture but stays faithful to its own proclamation. I have been very much impressed by Michael Buckley's observations about the origin of modern atheism. He suggests that the root of modern atheism rests in those theologians who, in an attempt to gain a hearing in non-religious circles, adopted rationalist methods and failed to proclaim faith. In our own day, we cannot expect to be true to ourselves, unless we remain steadfast in our witness to the Gospel, even as we take into account the secular environment in which we live and seek to engage it but do so as believers.

These convictions, in my estimation, give important directions to "Renew My Church." They also address in their own way the challenges of the social and cultural setting that Fr. Cameli describes. Ultimately, our movement forward as God's church depends on a reclaiming of our true identity as disciples of Jesus who are sent by him to be in mission to a world deeply in need of its Savior.

Conclusion

One of the unanticipated by-products of the "Renew My Church" process is the new life it is giving to our priests. As I call them to lead people in this time of discernment they understand that this will require that they be more in tune with the hidden moments of God's presence in their own life and ministerial experience. I have challenged them to take seriously their role of presbyter, a Greek word that means "elder" but also "one who goes before" or "takes precedence." This does not mean taking the first places of honor, but taking the lead as a scout, who for the people on pilgrimage risks crossing new frontiers, unafraid of threshold experiences.

"Renew My Church" will involve crossing some new thresholds, from past to future, from memory to dream, from facts to possibilities. All this will happen in a synodal church, that is, a church that travels on the road together—people, priests, and bishop. And everyone will sense that they are up to it, believing, as Pope Francis has said, that "we are not in an era of change but a change of era."

And even more, as Pope Francis has also said, everyone must be convinced that this renewal that goes forward in a synodal church is what God wants of us in this moment: "The world in which we live, and which we are called to love and serve, even with its contradictions, demands that the Church strengthen cooperation in all areas of her mission. It is precisely this path of *synodality* which God expects of the Church of the third millennium."[1]

[1] Address at Ceremony Commemorating the 50th Anniversary of the Institution of the Synod of Bishops, October 17, 2015.